In the Eye of the Wild

In the Eye of the Wild

NASTASSJA MARTIN

Translated from the French by Sophie R. Lewis

nyrb **New York Review Books** New York

This is a New York Review Book

published by The New York Review of Books

435 Hudson Street, New York, NY 10014

www.nyrb.com

Copyright © 2019 by Éditions Gallimard
Translation copyright © 2021 by Sophie R. Lewis
All rights reserved.

This work received support from the Cultural Services of the French
Embassy in the United States through their publishing assistance program.

Library of Congress Cataloging-in-Publication Data
Names: Martin, Nastassja, author. | Lewis, Sophie, translator.
Title: In the eye of the wild / by Nastassja Martin; translated from the
    French by Sophie Lewis.
Other titles: Croire aux fauves. English
Description: New York: New York Review Books, [2021]
Identifiers: LCCN 2021012498 (print) | LCCN 2021012499 (ebook) |
    ISBN 9781681375854 (paperback) | ISBN 9781681375861 (ebook)
Subjects: LCSH: Martin, Nastassja. | Bear attacks—Russia—
    Kamchatka—Anecdotes. | Anthropologists—Biography. |
    Human-animal relationships. | Nature—Effect of human beings on.
Classification: LCC QL737.C27 M352113 2021 (print) |
    LCC QL737.C27 (ebook) | DDC 599.7840957/7—dc23
LC record available at https://lccn.loc.gov/2021012498
LC ebook record available at https://lccn.loc.gov/2021012499

ISBN 978-1-68137-585-4
Available as an electronic book; ISBN 978-1-68137-586-1

Printed in the United States of America on acid-free paper.

1 2 3 4 5 6 7 8 9 10

To all creatures of metamorphosis,
both here and there.

"For I have been ere now a boy and a girl,
a bush and a bird and a dumb fish in the sea."
—EMPEDOCLES, *On Nature*, fragment 117

Autumn

THE BEAR LEFT SOME HOURS AGO now, and I am waiting, waiting for the mist to lift. The steppe is red, my hands are red, face swollen and gashed, unrecognizable. As in the time of myths, obscurity reigns; I am this blurred figure, features subsumed beneath the open gulfs in my face, slicked over with internal tissue, fluid, and blood: it is a birth, for it is manifestly not a death. Around me, wads of brown hair stiffened by dried blood litter the ground, proof of the recent combat. For eight hours, perhaps more, I've been hoping a Russian army helicopter will break through the fog to come and find me. I made a tourniquet for my leg with my rucksack strap when the bear took off, and Nikolai helped bandage my face when he reached me. He emptied our precious supply of *spirt* over my head, and it ran down my cheeks along with the tears and blood. Then he left me; he took my little fieldwork Alcatel to call the emergency services from the spur of an outcrop, thinking, inevitably, of the patchy network, the ancient phone, the far-off cell towers, praying they would all hold up, because all around rise the volcanoes that only a few moments earlier feted our freedom but now mark out our prison.

I am cold. I feel for my sleeping bag, wrap myself in it as best I can. My thoughts go out to the bear, then back to myself, building connections, analyzing and dissecting, fashioning a survivor's castles in the air. Inside my mind must look like a wild proliferation of synapses sending and receiving data more rapidly than ever, that is the pace of it: dazzling, lightning fast, unchecked, and ungovernable— the pace of dreaming, yet nothing has ever been more real or more immediate. The sounds I hear are enhanced, I hear like an animal, I am that wild animal. I wonder for a moment whether the bear will come back to finish me off, or to be killed by me, or indeed for us both to die in a final embrace. But already I know, I sense, that this will not happen; he is far away now, he is stumbling through the high steppe, blood dripping down his pelt. As he grows farther away and I look deeper into myself, we each regain our self-possession. He without me, I without him; how to survive despite what I have lost in the other's body, how to live with what has been left behind there.

I hear it long before it arrives. To Nikolai and Lanna who rejoined me a moment ago, it's inaudible. It's coming, I say, no nothing there, they reply, just us in the vast space with the mist that rises and falls. Yet a few minutes later an orange metal monster, a refugee from the Soviet era, comes to pluck us from this place.

•

It's night in Klyuchi, the solid depths of the night. *Klyuchi*—"key village," the training center, the Russian army's secret base in the Kamchatka region. I am not meant to know that it's at this poor strip of earth that Moscow is firing weekly missiles in order to measure their range and be ready to hit the Bering Strait's American coastline in the event of war. I am also not meant to know that all the indigenous peoples in the area, the Evens, Koryaks, and Itelmens, what's left of them, are recruited here, because without reindeer and without forest, absurdity is now the norm and it has come down to fighting on behalf of their tormentors. Except I do know it, and have known from the start; I know it because it's my profession to know these things. The Evens, whose lives in the forest I've been sharing for several months, have told me about the bombs that explode near their barracks in the evenings. They laughed at my questions, studied my face, often called me a spy, lightly, teasingly, ironically; they tried me out in every possible role but they never held anything back. The village; the drinking; the fights; the forest that is retreating, and with it their native tongue forgotten little by little; the lack of work; the homeland, their savior, which offers them the base at Klyuchi in return.

The irony of fate. The clinic is in this key village—this is where we land, behind the barbed wire and fences, behind the watchtowers, plumb into the lion's den. I who used to enjoy a private giggle at knowing all these top-secret things about this top-secret place now find myself actually inside the medical facility for the soldiers and wounded of the almost-war that quietly goes on here.

3

An old lady stitches up my wounds. I watch her handle the needle and thread with infinite care. I have passed through the pain stage, I feel nothing now, but I'm still awake, I don't miss a stitch, I am lucid beyond my human senses, detached from my body while still within it. *Vs'o budet khorosho*, everything will be fine. Her voice, her hands, that's all. I see my long blond and red hair fall in clumps at my feet as she cuts it off so she can sew up the slashes on my head, which by some miracle has not been crushed. I struggle to discern a light but there's nothing to be done, the night's depths are opaque, filled with pain, endless, there's no relief that way. Then I see him. The fat, sweaty man who has just come into the room is waving his phone at me, he is taking a photo, he means to immortalize this moment. So horror does have a face, and it's not mine but his. I am enraged. I want to throw myself at him, tear his paunch open, rip out his guts, and nail his damn phone to his hand so he can take the sweetest selfie of his life while taking his leave of it—but I can't. I can only mumble at him to stop, and awkwardly try to hide my face; I am broken, shattered. The old lady understands; she pushes him outside and locks the door. People, she says, you know how they are.

The rest of the night goes on like that, with her, I am stitched, washed, cut, stitched again. I lose my sense of time, it runs on, we're floating together on a dark ocean infused with alcohol, carried by a swell that builds and falls away. Around midday the next day they come to collect me, the helicopter is here, I'm to be transferred to Petropavlovsk. A Russian done up as a firefighter steps out, tall,

4

smiling, crimson-uniformed and reassuring. He offers me a wheel-chair; I refuse, stand, hold onto his shoulder to go down the steps, white grey white grey, through the door, and we're on the concrete forecourt. Here, people swarming to see the show are at the ready with their phones. With my free hand I hide my face again, avoid the flashes, and, supported by my rescuer, vanish once again into the belly of the helicopter.

•

I spend the flight semiconscious; I remember being cold and struggling to breathe, my throat full of blood. When we land the doctors make me lie on a stretcher, on my back. I tell them I can't, I can't breathe like that, but they persist, several of them come to hold me down, it's as though the entire staff is there, and I am choking. There are shouts, screams, I feel a needle prick in an arm I can't move, then suddenly everything stops, the lights dance, I lose consciousness for the first time since the bear, nothing more, nothing at all, space, a blank, no dreams.

When I wake I am completely naked, alone, strapped to the bed. Restraints grip my wrists and ankles. I examine the situation. I am in a vast and decrepit white room, empty beds are lined up beside mine. It looks like one of those old clinics from Soviet times. Voices echo faintly. A tube runs into my nose and down my throat; it takes me a long while to realize why I am breathing so strangely and that it's this green-and-white plastic thing stuck to my neck: a tracheotomy. In my mild delirium, I expect to see Doctor Zhivago pop up at any moment; the film set is ready. But it's a blond nurse who comes in, smiling. Nastinka, you'll come through this, she says. Behind her, a tall, stocky man appears, his boots resounding on the floor tiles; gold chain, gold teeth, gold watch. He's the head doctor and it shows; it's he who's in charge of future and current operations, he who is behind my strait-jacket and everything else. Get in his good books, my first thought.

He is friendly enough, with his gilded lord-of-the-hospital smile. He compliments me: No one understands how it's possible you're alive, but you are—bravo. *Molodets*. You're a very strong woman, he adds. I reply that I'd just like my straps to come off. We can't do that, it's not possible, you stay this way, it's to protect you from yourself. Oh, right. The two days that follow are torture. The tube in my throat is appallingly painful and the smiley first nurse has disappeared; another one, younger, looks after me—too young. The head nurse keeps a vague eye on her, they do have to learn . . . This novice becomes my worst nightmare. I'm obsessed: all I can think about is how to get free of this prison of straps. As soon as my guardians disappear through the door, I start dreaming up impossible strata-gems. Twice I succeed in releasing myself, I pull out the tube which conveys brown-and-black mash to my stomach—I remember that color. Time for the feed, I hear shouted along the corridors at the end of the day. Have you done the feed? the head nurse asks her apprentice. The word is "feed"—*kormit*. I can see my old friend Ilo, in his yurt in Manas, calling to his nephew Nikita: Have you fed the dogs? Go feed the dogs! *Idi kormit!* Ever since, I cannot hear that word without a spasm from deep in my stomach. I clearly remember the spiteful black eyes of that girl, scarcely more than a child, her malevolent stare. I can still see her injecting the food down my tube with a single plunge, wanting to punish me, to take revenge, for my existence, for her own miserable life, I don't know, for everything that will not obey, everything that stands up to her; she makes it clear that for this once, she has the power.

Poured suddenly, brutally, into my stomach, the mash makes me scream with pain. Tears stream down my cheeks; I have never been so powerless, at the mercy of men, women, and even kids; stripped, strapped down, stuffed, I am at the frontier of humanity, at what feels like the very edge of what a person can stand. Alerted by my cries, the head nurse returns, comes over, and scolds her junior, who flashes me a murderous look. It seems they'll make me pay dearly for my survival in woman-versus-bear. Does it hurt? asks the nurse. Yes! I say with all the conviction I can muster, in the hope she will give me something, anything, a drug to attenuate my pain a little. Chin up, *poterpi*, she says, and goes back to her paperwork. *Poterpi*, too, I can no longer stand to hear.

After the episode with the mash, I decide to lay down my arms— or to surrender, for I have no choice. I focus on being as good as gold, not protesting, asking for nothing and expecting nothing, tolerating the pain, the tube, and all the rest, until it's done with, or rather until something is done. If it weren't for the music that echoes around the room, so that every three seconds there's a drumroll followed by a single short beat, symphonic wallpaper, I'd have an easier time concentrating on the circumstances of my subjugation. On inquiring about the nature of this repetitive symphony, I learn that a very old but highly respected scientific study showed that this requiem, played on a loop, helped patients not forget to breathe: rrrrrrroooooooolllllll Klang! rrrrrrroooooooolllllll Klang! And we breathe—of course. At the heart of the Russian healthcare system am I. An idiosyncrasy of Russia's Far East, still mired in antique habits? I doubt that intensive care patients at Moscow hospitals are listening to the same tune as me. On the other hand, they aren't lying here in this clinic, with its gulag styling. I reflect that no one will believe me when I tell them about this when I get out, if I get out. I decide to write it all as soon as I can.

Fortunately my nights are more entertaining, though no less surreal. Annia follows Inna, then Yulia takes the baton. Every evening is the same. The nurse keeping watch sits at a low schoolchild's desk, at the end of the room. In the semidarkness, a minuscule night-light illuminating her work, she makes compresses. She cuts and folds, cuts and folds. Nothing here can be taken for granted. Everything is made by women's hands. Every night around the same time, the watching nurse's name rings from the next room, a man is calling. Annia! Casually she stands, glances at my bed, then steps through the door. I needn't listen for long to understand what's afoot. Barely stifled moans reach me, and masculine grunts; the head doctor is getting lively with his nursing staff. It's the same game every night, only the name changes: Yulia! Inna! It follows. The first time I saw the head doctor kiss one of my nurses on the lips in the middle of the day (albeit there was plainly no one but me in the intensive care unit to stand witness) I naively thought she must be his partner, a doctor and a nurse, why not, after all. Realizing that every nurse was kissing the head doctor on the lips as a matter of course, I then decided it must be a local custom: Evens from the same family will kiss each other on the lips in greeting. But when the moaning was repeated night after night, the world I'd dreamed up took a hit. It must have to do with some other undocumented custom. What a racket! And along with these sexual realizations, my own human life came to the fore again and I surfaced from my limbo; how strange to regain one's sense of self by listening to others make love every night. My suffering began to diminish.

Satisfied by my docility over the last few days, the nurses free my limbs, at last. You won't pull out the tube? No I won't pull anything out, I shall merely touch my bare body to remember how it feels. That day, I celebrate another triumph too: the nurse agrees to turn off the breathing symphony. It is a liberation.

Other doctors (male) come to see me, accompanied unfailingly by the head doctor who, delighted by this good behavior, watches over his survivor like a hawk. We talk, I lying on the bed, pulling my skimpy sheet as high as I can to hide my chest; they at my side or by my feet. Clearly, I am mending. Of course, they still refuse to give me my belongings, especially my phone; that's not allowed in this unit, they claim. I explain that I'm bored stiff. Don't you have anything to give me to pass the time, anything at all, a book perhaps? One of the doctors considers, then comes back with a book of jokes about the Russian medical profession, patients and staff. The cover is black, the text printed large; I don't remember the title. Sorry, this is all I have here . . . he seems embarrassed. No problem, this is just right, actually; I'll take it, I say.

They can't get over it. Nastinka is reading, five days after waking up, five days after her battle with the bear, she's reading. And jokes, too! Word must have got out, for a veritable parade now comes trotting through my room. They come to see me deep in the book, they ask if it's funny; very, I reply every time. They come to say hello and congratulate me. Towards the end of the next day, the head doctor appears, pushing a small television on wheels. Here you go, he says. Now you can look at something more interesting!

The nurse sets it up at the foot of the bed, turns it on randomly, and leaves me alone facing the little screen. Incredulous, I stare at the images that succeed each other without it at first sinking in; it's so bizarre, I can't bring myself to see what I am seeing. The first film I am shown in Petropavlovsk's crumbling intensive care unit tells the story of Nastinka (this is her name in the story), who is looking for her lover in the forest and can't find him; she calls and calls, but how is she to know that, fallen victim to a curse, the man she seeks has been transformed into a bear? She doesn't recognize him when eventually she does reach him. Unable to make her see him, to see who he really is inside, he dies of grief.

I go into a daze before this Little Red Riding Hood who shares my name, pursued by this bear lover who can no longer speak to her; she too unwittingly pursuing this bear, unaware that the man she loves has already metamorphosed. They are condemned to live in different worlds, they can no longer communicate. Their souls, or whatever is inside them, are henceforth imprisoned in skins that are *other*, that no longer correspond to the same expressions of life. I think of my own story. Of my Even title, *matukha*.* Of the bear's kiss on my face, his teeth closing over me, my jaw cracking, my skull cracking; of the darkness inside his mouth, the moist heat and the pressure of his breath, the grip of his teeth letting go; of my bear who abruptly, inexplicably changes his mind: his teeth will not be the cause of my death, he will not eat me.

A tear drops onto my cheek, my refreshed eyes continue to stare at the screen, which does no more, now, than reflect my own life. I am staring into a mirror. There is no more absurdity, no more strangeness or lucky coincidence. There is only resonance.

At this juncture the nurse comes in, glances my way, sees the tears in my vacant eyes, and turns to the screen. She purses her mouth, annoyed. This is unfortunate, she says. Silence. Shall I turn it off? She turns it off.

•

Because the bear went off with a chunk of my jaw clenched in his own, and because he broke my right zygomatic bone, they will have to operate on me again, soon. When I came in, they pinned a plate

*The feminine epithet *matukha* means "she-bear."

into the bone to hold up the lower right mandibular ramus; now my cheekbone must be reset. Why this wasn't done before is a mystery, but the head doctor assures me this morning that after this I will be able to leave the intensive care unit, to breathe normally; I could even "eat by myself," he adds, smiling.

For several days now I have been asking for my things, especially my phone, so I can call my family—without success. But that day, the head doctor's assistant bursts in and marches towards me. Do you know a Charles? Hope revives there and then; my words tumble out as I try to explain. Charles, my research partner, my friend, my workmate at the social anthropology lab; Charles, who came, too, on my first visit to Kamchatka; Charles, who must be so worried, so worried about me by now. Tell him I am OK, tell him I'm not dead, tell him . . . He cuts me off. Next time he calls, we'll tell him.

The next day the phlegmatic assistant returns. We have spoken to Charles. He says your mother and brother are on their way. Tears of joy trickle over my swollen, stitched-up face, which must be shining like a setting sun; I have been hoping so hard for them to come, I have called out to them so often, sending my heart's silent words over land and ocean. My poor mother. Who worried so much about her daughter always traveling to Lord knows where these past fifteen years, to Alaska, to Kamchatka, into the mountains and forests or under the sea, so often caught up in unstable and perilous situations;

my lovely mother, for once I accede to all her motherly anxiety: perhaps she wasn't wrong. From my bed in this dilapidated room, I put myself in her shoes, and it's even worse, almost untenable; for the sake of my own survival, I must stop my plunge into her mother's heart, otherwise I'm sunk. I recall clearly something she said just before I went back into the field this year, words spoken without a smile, with the authority of a mother who knows her daughter is tearing herself in two, being sucked in by that other world that means nothing to her mother, but whose power, influence, and fascination she can feel. A mother whose daughter inevitably defends herself: "I'm an anthropologist," she keeps saying, I am not infatuated, I'm not losing myself in the field, I'm still me—everything you tell yourself because otherwise you'd never go. My mother, then, who said, several months before all of this: If you don't come back this time, I shall be coming to look for you. Knowing that she's somewhere between France, Siberia, and Kamchatka, my heart is bursting with joy and sorrow at once. I think about Niels coming with mother. My elder brother, who plays the protector; my brother who, despite his tall frame, has always been more fragile than I; my colossus with his feet of clay, an unwitting titan of feeling and sensitivity—luckily Maman is there for him, I think. She will always be the toughest of us three. My mother has come through other wars and, even if no one yet knows for sure, this is one that will end in birth, not death.

That night, my last in the intensive care unit, strange screams enliven the darkness. They've picked someone up in the street who is very drunk, unimaginably drunk. Or perhaps he handed himself in, who knows. Anyway, now he is in the room next door. I hear him, I listen, it's a dizzying litany that kicks off then and continues uninterrupted until dawn. The duty nurse has exchanged the head doctor's fat hands for new insults: howling in the corridors and untrammeled obscenities. A door slams, the man next door finds he is locked in—and he begins to sing. A long, melancholy song, telling of the good old times; the *kolkhoz* farms; the Red Army; the cows, milk, reindeer; the books and films; the animal skins and the trading posts; the vodka. I should like to see his face, to see the pain that makes his voice shake between sobs. What is this world he mourns? How old can he be, to mourn these bygone times? I picture him, bottle in hand a few hours earlier, weaving amid the muddy potholes of one of the town's deeply rutted streets, in the bleak strip-lighting of one of those supermarkets that sprang up less than five years ago, sprouted there in the midst of those Soviet housing blocks with their cracks running from top floor to basement, bearing witness to a world that has changed too much, too fast and that is already decaying before even arriving at its predatory maturity.

I listen to my neighbor's ravings and I am transported to the yurt in Tvayan. Again I see old Vasya just before sunrise, sitting on a reindeer skin, his eyes half closed; most likely he is still in that liminal place that precedes our waking, where dreams retain their power over our bodies. *Kolkhoz direktor, krasnaya armiya, sovkhoz direktor*, over and over. Kolkhoz director, Red Army, state farm director, he repeats tirelessly, rocking gently in the dawn light that reaches in through the roof. I remember being struck by the force of the impact, of the collision, between the yurt's semicircle, the campfire's flames that told of the invisible world, which Vasya himself would translate of an evening into a few words, softly spoken, and Soviet modernity, which has penetrated to the heart of the dreams dreamt by the furthest, the strangest, the least prepared of all human peoples. A story is brewing in Vasya's labyrinths. A scrap of memory, a flash of an encounter, a fragment of a moment? I don't know if my fellow patient in the intensive care unit is Even, Itelmen, Koryak, or Russian, but I do know that he dwells on the same burdens of the past as my old friend in Tvayan.

•

My last operation is today. There is quite a crowd around my bed. The mood is festive. There are at least ten of them, doctors and nurses, here to officiate or just to observe, they chat with me, they're cheery. You know you'll be out of here in no time and then you're off to the ordinary hospital? one of them remarks while preparing the anesthetic. The head doctor makes his entrance, collar unbuttoned, chest hair and all his gold chains out to play. This is going to go fine, he says, rolling up his sleeves. Bright gold smile and a wink. Then, for the second time since the bear, the lights begin to dance.

When I wake up, for a moment I think I'm still sedated and dreaming, so bizarre is what meets my eyes. All the beds around mine have been pushed away and a Russian rock and roll track is echoing around the room. There's no one else now except the nurse, who is dancing with her mop and singing at the top of her voice. I begin to laugh. Nastya, you're awake! she yells at me. That's it you're out of here today's the day you're leaving come on now pull yourself together a bit they'll soon be here to collect you!

Later the head doctor returns. It went well, he says, I've done what was required, you'll even be able to eat. No more tube; yes, it's true. No more trach either, just a bandage over the hole in my neck. I can't get over it, I am happy as I've never been before. Someone is waiting for you outside, he adds. But who? My family already? But it's too soon . . . No, he breaks in. Someone . . . and he makes a circular gesture with his hand, indicating his own face with a grimace. Someone tanned? I try to translate. Dark? Yes, dark. He's there, he's waiting at the exit and wants to see you.

The stretcher-men come, we rattle out of my cell, for the first time I see the networks of corridors, the furniture, the other rooms, the places I pictured throughout my long nights. No trace of last night's singer; a shame, I think, I glance into the room he was singing from, but it's empty, the bedsheets are off and rolled into a ball at the foot of a mattress, also tossed to the floor. Now the exit is so close, light floods my stretcher, the first face to welcome me into the day is Andrey's. I want to hold him tight, to weep, to tell him the whole story, but already the nurses are carrying me away from him, from his benevolent gaze, the gaze of a friend.

I'll be waiting in your room, he calls to me as I go by.

•

Andrey must be feeling a bit guilty. Yet it would be too simple if everything really were his fault, as Daria was to claim a few days later. But to absolve him completely by classing him as extrinsic to the circumstances of my fight would not be fair either. I see myself again in the yurt at Mil'kovo, shortly after I arrived that summer,

16

four years ago; fever had confined me to the bed of skins, reliant on Andrey and his herbal infusions. The place is taking hold in you, you'll be stronger afterwards, he had said. I had spent two weeks, perhaps three, cloistered in the yurt with him, talking about animal spirits, about those that choose us even before we meet them. I recovered and was soon off and out again, he would have liked to have kept me so he could teach me more, but I thought only of the forest, the true forest, not the forest of the stories. I liked Andrey very much but I hated the village. I preferred to go and stay with Daria, and I gave Andrey no choice: I went to live with the Evens who had chosen a different life, far from the villages, far from tourism, far from the state. Andrey was constrained here, and, although he was as much an indigene as Daria and her family, as time went by, his sculpture studio had become more than a research subject for me; it felt like a decompression chamber between my world and theirs, whether I was leaving or returning.

But this time is different. I don't go home, I steer away from the woods, I'm heading for the mountains. Something tastes wrong, something crucial. He knows, he feels it. I remember the moment he gave me the claw, just as I was leaving. You know you are already *matukha*, I'm not telling you anything new. Take this with you when you're walking up there. I can hear his words, reminding me of our talks during my feverish wanderings and warning me against the bear's spirit that is following me, waiting for me, that knows me. Yet he does not try to hold me back. He doesn't raise a hand to stop me from climbing up to the volcanoes. And this is precisely Daria's charge: that he knew, about me, about the bear, and that he did nothing. That he's always done nothing, said nothing; or rather: that he said it all to a wild creature who would anyway, defiantly, race off to meet her ruin, anticipating her initiation, and that it would be a miracle if she were to survive. No, nothing is his fault. What he did was this: he guided my feet so that I could go to meet my own dream.

Daria, too, always knew. She knows who visits me when I'm asleep; I tell her in the early mornings about the bears of my night, familiar, hostile, comical, mean, affectionate, troubling. She listens in silence. She laughs, seeing me crouched among the blueberry bushes with my blond hair sticking out above the leaves; it's like you have fur, she tells me every time. She compares my wiry body with that of the she-bear; she wonders aloud which of us, woman or she-bear, sleeps in the other's den. But Daria has something that Andrey does not, that Andrey will never have: she is a mother. A woman who has known pain in her own flesh, who knows life and death, and who, more than anything in the world, wants to protect those she loves and spare them suffering. Daria too can see into the two worlds. Yet she would never tear a child from his family's land; she would not take him to the forest, would not draw a circle around him saying you stay there, would not entrust him to the outside world for a moon's cycle to let him forge in his body the bonds that will make him a man later on. This is the father's role: to expel the child into the world once more. I've been without a father since adolescence. Andrey has, in a way, stepped into this vacancy, assumed the role of he who inducts by pushing the child beyond the soft and simple world of the uterus. It is for this reason that Daria will always hate him.

In the hospital room, Andrey settles in next to the plant by the window, on the little bed opposite the one on which the nurses help me to sit. We look at each other in silence, the door closes, we are alone. He says: Nastya, have you forgiven the bear? Silence again. You must forgive the bear. I don't reply straightaway; I know I have no choice, and yet for once I want to disobey, to reject fate, our bonds, to reject everything we move towards that is inexorable, I want to shout that I wish I had killed him, to expel him from my system, that I am so angry he has disfigured me like this. But I don't, I say nothing. I breathe. Yes. I have forgiven the bear.

Andrey looks away, at the floor, his long black hair falls to the left of his face, he waits like that for a moment, two tears drop onto the tiles. He looks up, his black eyes wet, shining, piercing. He didn't mean to kill you, he wanted to mark you. Now you are *medka*,* she who lives between the worlds.

•

There is a commotion in the corridor. Andrey stands, opens the door a little, looks out, turns back to me. They're here; stand up. I stagger to the doorway and lean on Andrey's shoulder; they come

*The Even word *medka* is used to indicate people who are "marked by the bear," having survived their encounter with one. From that time on, people called *medka* are considered to be half human, half bear.

in. She is first. Her disheveled blond hair scarcely hides her swollen eyes, reddened from a week of tears, sorrow, and fear. He follows behind. His lips trembling, jaw tense with anxiety and expectation. My mother hugs me with all the strength she has left, my brother puts his arms around us both and hides our wet faces from prying eyes. We are weeping together and it is now, at last, quite real. I am not myself anymore, my head is a ball scored with swollen red claw-marks and sutures. I am nothing like myself anymore, and yet I've never looked more like my own spirit; it has been imprinted on my body, the marks on my skin reflect both a journey out and a return.

Later on, my hospital room with its plant turns into a lab, people join me here who are so different you can hardly picture them side by side, in audience with she-who-did-battle-with-the-bear. Daria and her son, Ivan, have left their forest; her daughter, Yulia, has left her husband behind at the army camp in Vilyuchinsk in order to join them in Petropavlovsk. An odd new family comes together: my mother, my brother, and Daria and her children, the first occasion these people have ever been in the same space-time, all cast into this precarious, liminal zone. I have become an unlikely link, between these people as human beings and between them and the world of the bears up in the high tundra.

•

Later still, I am alone with Daria and Ivan. I ask, how did you know about the bear? You can't use a phone in the Tvayan forest. For a hundred kilometers around there isn't a single antenna, nothing. And for several months already, the radio that kept them in touch with the region's other hunting grounds had been out of order. Daria wipes the sweat dripping from her forehead with a tissue, rests her chin on clasped hands, lowers her voice, and begins the story of that particular day, the day when I was racing to meet my bear, the day when they were in their forest, far from the volcanoes.

They are in Cruxkatchan with the children, a few kilometers down the Icha River, south of Tvayan. They are fishing. Towards the end of summer there are always more salmon here than at the main hunting ground. Here they have nothing but a rudimentary cabin where everyone sleeps side by side, on skins on the ground. Just below this shelter, the river widens and grows stiller; it's an excellent spot to cast a line. While they are drinking their midafternoon tea, Ivan falls backwards and blacks out. Deeply worried, his mother gives him a good thump and he opens his eyes. After a few minutes, he sits up. Something's happened to Nastya, he says. He leaves the cabin, goes down to the river, starts up the motorboat, and heads for the camp at Manash', a hundred kilometers to the north, to climb up to the tree house where we make all our calls when we're in the forest. Sitting in the branches three meters up, cell phone pointed at the sky, he receives the message I asked Nikolai to write for me when I was still at Klyuchi, the key village. When I left the clinic, before stepping into the helicopter, I had given him my Russian phone, indicating he should call Ivan and Charles, the two men who looked after my two homes at the time, one back in France and one here in Kamchatka. I know I am going to put them through a nightmare, but the guilt has not kicked in. I know, though I didn't know why at the moment the bear and I collided, that this bear who is

21

mine first of all, is bound to us too, to all three of us. To them, and to me.

•

Thinking of Charles, I remember that day towards the end of the Evens' mourning, when we emerged from the forest. After three days of journeying between the hunting camps, after burying Daria's mother at Drakoon, after the tears the intensity the hollowness and daze, we reach Sanush', at the border station; it's the end of our very first field visit in the Icha River region. Charles and I go to wash farther along the river; we take a narrow path, branches catching at our faces and arms. We begin our ablutions as soon as we come to the water. A few seconds later a low growl reaches our ears. We both look up; the big white dog called Shaman who has become our companion bounds along the river. Charles looks at me and says, don't follow. I stand: his voice is so distant, almost muffled. All my senses attuned, I set off in pursuit of Shaman, the blood pulsing at my temple as it must pulse in his. I find him thirty meters downstream, poised by a line of trees on the bank overlooking the water, barking. I creep forward little by little behind him, almost crawling now, until at last I'm at his side. There, a few meters away, a colossal she-bear stands, one paw on a tree, the other dangling; she is panting in our direction. Two bear cubs romp behind her. My heart is exploding in my chest; I raise myself a little and gaze at her. She lets go of the tree, stands erect, and stares at us both, then gives a long uninflected growl. I look at the dog and the dog looks at me. I softly drop back down; I am out of sight, I turn and run as fast as I can to the water hole where I left Charles; get back to him fast, don't leave him alone there, that's all that's in my head. You saw her, he says, when I reach him. Yes, I reply, breathing hard. You're mad, he tells me once more. I know, and I'm smiling.

Later that night, words flow onto the page. I write and it's a flood, inevitable; I write because I am profoundly affected. I should say that I have two field notebooks. One is diurnal. It is filled with disparate notes, detailed descriptions, retranscriptions of dialogues and speeches, most of it impenetrable until I get home and put it in some kind of order, until I organize this mass of minute data into something stable, intelligible, something readable. The other notebook is nocturnal. Its content is partial, fragmentary, unstable. I call it the black book because I can't really define what it contains. The diurnal and nocturnal notebooks are the outward expressions of the dualism that consumes me, of a sense of the objective and the subjective that I hold onto in spite of myself. They are, respectively, the inward and the external: the one, a writing that comes unbidden, immediate, instinctive, untamed, with no purpose other than to reveal what passes through me, a report on body and mind at a given moment; and the other, paradoxically less guarded yet more controlled, to be reworked later into something reflective, that will finish up in the printed pages of a book. That night, of course, after the bear, it's the black book that I take up.

JULY 8, 2014

Once more those eyes that pierce right through, that fill memories with vivid, fleeting images. Constellation of details swarming in my body; flashes of colors that recall what the body's already lost of the shared presence of other creatures. Phantasm of a desire particular to the forests, to the solitary predators, to their rage, to their pride, and to their vigil. Tension of their unplanned encounters, unspeakable, improbable, in flux yet. As alone they lose their way, so alone they cut themselves off, and so alone they forget. Their eyes' meeting saves them from themselves by projecting them into the alterity of the being that looks back. Their eyes' meeting keeps them alive.

That night, closing the black book, I turn off my headlamp and stay there lying in the darkness with my eyes open, and listen to the breathing around me. What is happening? I remember this distress. I am becoming something I don't understand; it is speaking through me.

And of Ivan, my thoughts go back to our first encounter. The rain is torrential, Charles and I have just reached Manash' on the Icha, it is June 2014. We've been waiting in the yurt for three days for the weather to grow more settled so we can go on. I am deeply bored. I doodle on my notebooks: I can't find anything intelligent to say, I have no words in me and even less sense; in any case, nothing is happening that's worth writing about. The afternoon is almost over.

Ilo half-heartedly stirs the dogs' *apana,** which is simmering over the embers; the steam from the kettle rises slowly to the opening at the yurt's peak. Rain drums on the tent cloths, it's deafening, numbing. Quite distinctly, I see once more the yurt's free panel fly up to the left of the roof with a sudden flap, and the man in dripping orange oilskins who comes in. *Zdorovo*, he fires out, smiling. His eyes scan the yurt's occupants, note the two foreigners, pause on mine. Something has swept down on me, I think, and I hold his gaze.

•

Charles is not with us at Petropavlovsk and yet he is very present. He takes care of all the logistical phone calls, he translates the papers relating to the operations I've already undergone here, in Russia, and those for my upcoming transfer to a French hospital. He spends sleepless nights; I feel his pain in my heart. He calls me on my Russian phone, which I've managed to retrieve; he weeps into the handset, says over and over that I mustn't die, I can't die. I am not dead, I am born: I say this to him too, just as I say it to my mother, to my brother, who all reply yes yes, hoping that I'll soon see reason and forget these tales of mingled souls and spirit dreams. True, it's hard to explain. Because it's still confused in my head, I struggle to find the right words for what happened, for what is happening. I don't realize this at the time, but their incomprehension is just a tiny foretaste of that awaiting me in France.

*The *apana* is the meal the Evens feed their dogs. Everything not eaten by people goes into it: fish heads, bones, guts, leftovers, potatoes, etc. The *apana* stews on the fire all day.

Daria leaves me alone with Ivan. He holds me in his arms, cries softly on my shoulder, his tears running down my neck. Why didn't you listen when I asked you not to go? Why did you go up there when you could have stayed with us in Tvayan? The answer is the same, untranslatable into any language. I had to go to meet my dream. The same frustration.

A nurse comes in. Nastya, someone wants to see you. An agent from the FSB, Russia's Federal Security Service, follows her in: uniform, kepi, pistol on his belt. You will have to gather your strength for an interview, miss, he says, closing the door. Ivan is still here; he retreats until he has melted into the corner of the little bathroom at the back of the room. He crouches and vanishes into the shadow. I watch him and think of the day we said goodbye on the tundra at Sanush'. I won't be going any farther, he had said, although Lyuba, little Nikita, and I would continue our way on foot after two days by boat, in order to rejoin the road that would take us back, three hundred kilometers later, to the village of Mil'kovo. Just like today, in the dark corner between the basin and the shower, he had crouched down there in the ferns on the forest's lip, he'd taken out a cigarette and watched us walk on through the bare tundra towards that other world that was not his. For a long time we could see his still form keeping watch, then the tiny green dot that he'd become stood up and disappeared into the trees growing along the river.

The FSB man settles, like all the others before him, onto the little bed opposite mine, and the interrogation begins. He is here in order to understand two things: First, what a young Frenchwoman was doing in the environs of Klyuchi, the key military-base village, descending the icy slopes of a volcano with two Russians in her wake, entirely under her own steam. Second, how it was possible that this foreigner was able to survive a bear attack, witnesses having reported that she stabbed her attacker in the right flank with an ice ax while defending herself. The central question to resolve is the following: Is she a highly trained secret agent sent by France (or worse, by the US) to spy on Russia's military facilities in the region? The facts as they stand do not look favorable. The agent adds that his report also includes notes that I have spent some years working in Alaska before coming here; that I entered Kamchatka under a research visa, which in no way improves my case; that I have spent the majority of my time in a military no-fly zone in the south of the Bystrinsky region, where the last of the Even hunters still live an almost totally self-sufficient existence. In any case, what were you doing there? he asks me curtly. Ivan flattens himself even further behind the shower door. Research, I reply. Ethnographic research, I add. It takes the agent more than three hours to concur with me that I am not a spy and that, even though it's barely believable, I emerged alive from this business for reasons arising from neither war nor espionage.

•

In the days that follow, a strange procession begins. Humans have this curious mania for attaching themselves to the suffering of others, like oysters to their rocks. They carry on as if this event at last revealed their souls to them, as if this tragedy brought to the surface emotions long buried deep inside, in their vital organs, feelings so dazzlingly authentic that they become too much to bear alone. In order to shed these feelings, it seems the most convenient approach is to bring them straight back to the initiator of the inward disturbance. In this case, to me. So a number of strangers arrived at the door to my corridor, come to see me, to bring me a little something and to confide how they empathize with me in my suffering. Most of the time, I felt like screaming; I was boiling with frustration. Each time I wondered how the person failed to understand that a woman of twenty-nine who is suddenly disfigured might be wishing for seclusion, for serenity and silence? I begged the nurses to block my door to all comers; I pleaded with them to allow in only close friends and family. A demand that only added to my keepers' confusion, for my loved ones looked nothing like one another, spoke different languages, and came from altogether different worlds. One evening, the nurse who'd been bringing my kasha for the last week said, laughing: Nastya, you might almost say there are two different women occupying this room!

The time passes slowly. Each day, expert female hands undo the bandage wrapped around my head, they clean the stitches and rewrap the bandage. One of these afternoons, the kindest nurse gently strokes my head and says: Nastya, you will not be bald. I feel almost like laughing, it must be nerves. I hadn't realized that "being bald" was among my possible outcomes.

The postoperative analyses are good, and so we prepare to pack bags for the return to France. My mother and I spend hours, sitting side by side on my little bed, debating which hospital it would be better to have admit me, which maxillofacial department, under the care of which surgeons. We hesitate for some time, then opt for the Salpêtrière in Paris. My other brother, Thibaut, and my big sister, Gwendoline, live in Paris; Charles does too, and all three push for this decision in their phone calls. We ponder the gamut of arguments, weigh the pros and cons for hours at a time, and then let go. Like me, my mother hasn't the strength to think further ahead. Had I known, everything might have turned out differently. Or perhaps not. In any case, it's too late to go back.

•

The day we leave, an ambulance takes me to the airport. And I am made to wait inside the vehicle; the paramedics won't let me out. Outside, Daria and Ivan stand erect on the tarmac. I bribe my driver to let them come in, just for a moment. Favor granted. They come in and we weep. Then Daria pulls herself together, as she always does, she who knows the trials of life better than anyone. Again I see her lovely face above the fire in the yurt at Tvayan, one summer evening when the children are asleep on the skins and the grown-ups smoke outside and hold spirited discussions. Her voice low, she is practically whispering as she describes the loss of the two fathers to her five children, her two husbands who have not made it: the first, lost to the kolkhoz machine; the second, to the post-Soviet world of vicious brawling and petty banditry. I remember I was alarmed by the violent deaths she described; I felt like crying when, every time she caught sight of a bear, she wondered whether it might not be her second husband, carried off by the waves and now come back to see her; and I remember thinking, inevitably, of my own lost loved ones, wondering where they were now and if they too could see me. Today, just as she did that evening, she repeats: *Ne nado plakat', Nastya.* You mustn't cry. *Vso budet khorosho.* Everything will be fine. And also: If we're to go on living, we mustn't think about the bad things. It's only love that we must remember.

•

Of the plane I have only brief and mostly rather unpleasant memories. Apart from the pain arising from my injuries, I recall more than anything an intense frustration: to travel first-class, which had never happened to me before, without being able to touch the champagne or smoked salmon, while beside me my brother enjoys a feast. My scar reopens due to the cabin pressure and blood drips down my right cheek. A tear runs down my mother's cheek. She takes out a tissue and dabs gently at the drops of blood. She is so strong, I think then. A scene from Moscow: a man of about fifty pushes my wheelchair (Maman has insisted that I "not cause a ruckus, for once" and that I stay sitting calmly, even if I'd have preferred to walk), so, curiosity piqued by my face, which is mostly covered by a brightly colored shawl tied Tuareg-style, this man asks: You're on your way back from Kamchatka...did you fall off a mountain? I savor a well-deserved little silence before replying: No, I had a fight with a bear.

Winter

THE SALPÊTRIÈRE, THEN. How to marshal the images of this place that should have been my refuge but turned out to be the nadir of my sojourn in hell? Chronologically, perhaps. They'd hardly left my room before I was in the bathroom, undoing the bandage around my head. I hadn't yet seen it. The gauze falls to the orangey linoleum. I stare down at it. Then I dare; I look up gradually, I stare into the mirror. My hair has been shaved like a boy's, it's almost a crew cut. The red scars across my face are still a bit swollen, while those on my scalp are beginning to disappear beneath the dark fuzz that's growing back. I drop to the floor and let my tears wash everything else away. I weep like a little girl left alone, I weep for all that had to happen, I weep for my bear, for my old, lost face, for my previous life, which too is certainly lost, I weep for everything that will never be the same again. I run my palm over my shaved head. At the touch, I feel that funny tickling along my scalp that makes you want to do it again and again. I stir myself: back to life. I get up, look in the mirror once more, look away, turn the bathroom door handle, and decide to brave the hospital with this face.

•

As it's a bear that has alighted at the Salpêtrière, traveling by way of my body, and a Russian bear, to boot, the hospital staff have activated all their safety and security procedures: I am in quarantine. The potted plant and kasha of Petropavlovsk are a distant memory; they don't mess around when it comes to hygiene and security here. Every time the nurses come in, they cover up with blue paper overalls that they throw away when they leave. The paper is actually a nonwoven fabric—my mother's partner points this out, because he worked in the industry for many years. And my guardians also put on gloves, and overshoes, and masks. They instruct my family to do the same, but luckily they won't comply; they resist the violence of the non-woven stuff and the masks, for my sake. I feel like a wild animal that's been trapped and pinioned under bright white lights to be examined in microscopic detail. Everything in me screams; the white halogen glare is scorching my eyes and skin. I want to disappear, to go back to the Arctic night, without sun or electricity. I remember the candles. It would be so much easier if I could just hide, hide, hide. I rally at nightfall, when they finally turn all the lights off, when the comings and goings stop. I stare deep into the darkness, I go underground, and speak to my bear.

•

During visiting hours I have visitors, especially at first. My brother Thibaut tells me about the documentaries he has directed most recently, he shows me clips and brings me passion fruit shakes. As for my sister, Gwendoline, to keep me company she has uprooted her office so that, for a few hours a day, she works from the corridors of the Salpêtrière. I hear her heels tapping outside my door as she paces up and down, earbuds in, doubtless making very important decisions on behalf of the national railroad authority. Charles also visits regularly. The first time, he brings me a postcard signed by everyone at the social anthropology lab. Each time thereafter, he describes the proceedings of the latest interesting lectures he's seen and relays run-ins between colleagues at the lab. I listen as if I were behind glass; his voice sounds far away. I picture myself on a vessel with the moorings unfastened, I am watching the shore slip farther and farther away. My boat is floating away on the current, stern first; I can still see the shapes of my family left behind on the land, but I am unable to stop or even reduce the distance that's growing between us.

Until the day I ask Charles to stop visiting, which makes him sad. I suspect he thinks I'm being unfair. I am sorry—is all I manage to say. I don't come up with any justification, nothing specific or rational comes to mind, no good reason. I am, quite simply, cutting myself loose. Not just from him, but from all my friends. I stop answering my phone.

•

I am an academic, I do understand. The need to share your work with students, to have them take part, to take advantage of every opportunity to further their knowledge, to debate interesting issues arising from a specific case. Except that today, I am the case. A long procession of medical students troops into my room, following their teacher like bees after their queen. They are my age, or almost, and with their notebooks in hand, their white lab coats and studious gazes, they observe me and listen to the professor describe my condition. Bear bite to the face and head, fracture of the lower right mandibular ramus, fracture of the right cheekbone, a number of lacerations to the face and head, another bite on the right leg. While they take notes I look at them one by one. They are so clean, so nicely lined up, so luminous in their white coats, I think. And I? I think again of the ill-judged words of a relative come to visit shortly after I arrived: It could be worse, you just look like you're fresh out of the gulag. Overwhelming urge to hide, to cover my face with a veil, remove myself from their eyes. I hear them, in the evening, telling their friends the story of the "bear girl" repatriated to their maxillofacial surgery unit. I try to silence the remarks I can already imagine. She is disfigured, poor thing. She must have been pretty —before.

•

The next day the hospital's therapist comes by. Low, square-heeled shoes, belted skirt, white lab coat, blond hair up in a chignon. Hello, Madame Martin, and the usual formalities that follow. She asks how I am feeling "psychologically." For want of anything better to say, I reply that my psyche is surely looking much like my bones and skin: torn, smashed, shredded. Anything else? I feel alive, I add, trying to smile. She considers me with a look that is meant to be kindly and full of goodwill. But really, how are you feeling? she asks again. A silence, then she goes on: Because, you know, the face is our identity. I look back at her, aghast. Thoughts collide in my head; I'm suddenly overheating. I ask her if she offers this kind of information to all the patients at the Salpêtrière's maxillofacial clinic. She raises her eyebrows, disconcerted. I want to explain that I've spent years collecting accounts of the multiple presences that can coexist within a single body, precisely in order to subvert this concept of singular, uniform, unidimensional identity. I also want to tell her how damaging it could be to issue such a judgment when the person in front of you has lost that aspect which, for better or worse, did indeed reflect a kind of unity, and is trying to reassemble herself with the elements of something *other*, which have now become part of her face. Except I keep that to myself. I manage only a polite: I think it's a bit more complicated. And also—but this just slips out: Lucky you can't open the windows in here . . . lost identity is a heavy sentence for a disfigured person. Against all expectation, she grants me a fresh smile—she likes a joke; it's a good sign, she must be thinking. She won't be thrown off course: Am I able to sleep at night? I guess she would like me to tell her the whole story—to describe the horror: the beast, its jaws, teeth and claws, and all the rest. My turn to crack a smile. She means well, and she's surely not incompetent either, she's just a bit off the mark, misguided. She makes wide, astonished eyes at me when I assure her that everything is much better at night. It's true: at night I see more clearly, because I am seeing beyond—beyond what is presented to my senses by daylight.

Do I have dreams? How to explain. Yes, all the time. But I do something else before dreaming—I remember. I replay the scene every evening before going to sleep: the weeks and hours that led up to the crisis of my life.

•

We are putting up the tent in a small clearing, having spent the day walking through the forest, machetes at the ready. Earlier, in the morning, we left the trail that had turned into a hairline path before vanishing into impenetrable undergrowth. Only tomorrow will we be above the brush; then we'll leave Klyuchi and its vast taiga behind, and climb straight up towards the volcanoes at last. Now and then, the snow-covered peaks show clear in the distance. We finish setting up our camp for the night, then we light a big fire and our shadows dance over the trees all around. It's the first day of our expedition on the massif of Klyuchevskaya, Kamchatka's highest volcano, a journey that should take a fortnight. That night, I go to sleep thinking of the mountains so close by, but my sleep brings me bears. They prowl by the tent, circling around the fire. They loom tall, brown, and ominous. I awake sweating and panicked. I thought I'd left these visions behind in the forest; I'd wanted to be rid of them but they were following me even here—so be it. For the next two days I have a stomachache, walk and walk, stop thinking about it. And then they go. The night visions always go in the end; you forget about them, that's all, which does not mean they cease to exist somewhere.

The vegetation is thinning; there are no more trees, and we are working our way through tall ferns. A three-hundred-meter climb, and we are pushing through dense alders. Our advance party is patently nonhuman, the scout is a bear: we can see its spoor running ahead of us and its scat full of berries. Another five hundred meters and the vegetation disappears, and the tracks too. At last, I think. We are leaving the evergreen, ever-living world behind. The view is mineral and unobstructed; there isn't another living thing between us and the horizon, only Nikolai and Lanna walking down below, hunched forward under their heavy packs. *Now* I can breathe, and

I shout my joy into the wind. This goes on for a few days, the smile on my lips, the lightness, my body attuning, my senses sharpening as we climb higher. There is an intoxication among the highest mountains, an intense joy peculiar to this detachment. And then, every time, comes the ordeal, following right behind it.

Lanna's backpack is too heavy for her. Nikolai and I made it as light as we could by sharing her load, but now we're out of space. In order to reach the col, more than three thousand meters up, between the Kamen and Klyuchevskaya volcanoes, I lay my pack on a rock, go back down, and carry hers up for her. We go on like this, in two-hundred-meter stages. What kind of insanity have I signed up for? I start to feel a nub of irritation deep in my belly, despite the breath-taking landscape, despite the freezing air revitalizing my flesh. After ascending Kamen, when we reach the col, a storm closes over us. We wait for three, four days, for the fog to lift so we can descend the glacier, but nothing changes. Our provisions have been calculated to last a little over two weeks; if we don't move tomorrow we won't have enough food to make it back. We are still enveloped in white, but my decision is made: we are leaving. In the early morning, I rope up Nikolai and Lanna, get the GPS out, select the next waymark, and peer deep into the fog layered below us. Much snow has fallen, and the crevasses are partly covered. I begin the descent with care, making my way through the murky air. Tighten the rope! I can hear the arcs of snow collapsing under my feet. Tighten the rope! I yell into the thick mist, and a slight new tension in the shoulder harness indicates that thirty meters up, Nikolai has understood and has

pulled the rope in a little. Right, left, right, forward; I avoid everything that could be a dip, I am zigzagging. The progress is slow but
we are descending, when suddenly the fog disperses. The snowfall
grows lighter, now it's drizzling over the glacier, which is muddy
with volcanic ash. The crevasses appear, distinct at last; I breathe
more freely.

What follows is a kind of Minotaur's labyrinth: a maze of hellish
valleys of exploded ice and lava. I find my way without too much
thought; I move like water, trying to take the easiest route. My feet
sink into the ash and I skid on sheets of black ice, but I am not
thinking about it; I'm recalling all the tiny things in life, occasional
winks from lovers, my friends' laughter. Mostly I crack jokes when-
ever we pause for a rest. Nikolai and Lanna watch me, uneasy, but
I manage to get a few smiles out of them. Humor is an unbeatable
remedy in extreme situations: it is part of surviving. After thirty
hours of nonstop descent, we finally leave the chaos behind. Below,
there is still a raging glacial river to be crossed, five meters wide and
a meter fifty deep, its waters vanishing into the crevasses downstream. We make it over despite a few disagreements; fear makes
our voices harsh. On the other shore, we all feel the desperate desire
to lie down and not move again. That evening, the last of my life
before, I question the rationale behind this expedition, intended as
a brief respite from the forest. I am drained, exhausted. We get out
the *spirt* and the little glasses. Inside our tent, plumb in the middle
of the glacial moraine, we drink a toast: well played, we'll be out
soon. That night I hardly sleep. Have to get out of here, fast. Get
back to life below. Leave these deadly heights.

•

I am walking in my wild form on the high plain. It is the end of our expedition; the volcano is disappearing into mist, the glacier reaches out its last crevasses, now there are just surface cracks. Our pace is unhampered, supple and quick; now we just have to get there. I remember how my mind boiled furiously just then, right after I untied Lanna and Nikolai. They irritated me with their lofty sentiments, even more wide-eyed now, right after our ordeal, with their witty words about the beauty of nature, about the landscape at last spread before our eyes since the cloud cap lifted and we put that hell of glaciers and volcanoes well and truly behind us. I watch Lanna in ecstasies and remember how she was two days before, in the fog, eyes full of tears as I held the rope taut so she could climb across the crevasses that were impossible to go around. I'm fuming inside. I pack the rope quickly as I can and free myself from them at last; I'm off the hook, such a joy, such lightness. I will not walk with them, perhaps because they're too slow and their conversations don't interest me, but mostly because I want to be able to sink into my thoughts. I point out our next landmark: the nice, distinctly visible great rock where we'll meet up. It's easy, it's straight ahead, there's nothing more to worry about, I tell them. I walk on alone; I'm almost running. I can see the forest, the tea steaming in the yurt, the embers' glow on oval faces and the hunter's green eyes. I can't wait. I'm fizzing; I am this desperate, so desperate to remove myself from the outside world. Or rather, from the landscape; it's this land that I want to get away from. From the theory that keeps Lanna and Nikolai walking, when their bodies and the pressure of the elements finally leave them in peace; from this notion that makes them go on yattering all day, eyes fixed on the sky. And yet, when I leave the mineral world behind, in running away from my rope team, I also go wrong; I too indulge in a kind of morbid contemplation—although it's not the peaks or the ground that I look to, it's what's inside, within myself. I am so desperate to get out of this landscape and back to the heart of the forest that I forget where I am, in a world that may be inhabited and crisscrossed by other creatures too. I forget, it's as simple as that. How could I forget? Even today I wonder. It was the glacier behind me, Nikolai and Lanna's Mother Nature and the scree as far as the eye could see; it was the last few days of blizzard, being stuck in our tent on the col, and the fear of being unable to make it back down from the volcanoes. It was that crazed river higher up that almost swept us away, the forced pace, and then the release when we were out of danger. It was the fatigue, the anxiety and tension, and the great tangle of it dissolving in one go. It was my inner darkness, which even the most remote expedition has not been able to cure.

It was all this at once, but those were not the reasons for my forgetting; they were only the circumstances. The true reasons belong to my dreams and can only be grasped fleetingly, in the darkest hour of the night.

Yes, I will try to tell you my dreams, I say to the therapist. Come back another time, it could be a long session. Apologetic smile. She's a bit inept, it's true. Annoying, too. But fundamentally, I think I rather like her even so. I like the way she squints and frowns; it's clear she wants to understand. I blame myself for not being nicer. I'll make up for it later, I tell myself, listening to the dull tapping of her heels on the green linoleum as she leaves, and then I am drawn to the window and my eyes are lost in branches as the trees sway gently outside.

•

It's the day of my first operation in France. My surgeon and her team are agreed that it would be risky to leave an ex-Soviet plate in my jaw—and safer to replace it with a Western one. The X-rays show my plate has been secured with screws that are much too big; "Russian-style" is the expression used. To make matters worse, the plate is very broad, they say, and positioned at such an angle as to make rehabilitation a risky venture. Perhaps at this point I ought to have spoken up to say that I for one was happy to trust the Russians, that I'd rather go home first and take some time to recover. I don't know. At this point, neither truth nor fairness are available to me. But are they ever? So it is that, calmly, remorselessly, my jaw is made the scene of a Franco-Russian medical cold war.

As I am wheeled back up from the operating table, the pain is intense. I ask for morphine for the first time, as I will do every evening after the operation, when the agony becomes unbearable. On a scale of one to ten, how much does it hurt? The famous question familiar to all hospital patients is addressed to me. At first I hesitate, stammer something; I'm afraid of overdoing it, afraid of making myself look weak. I mull over this peculiar scale and I make them explain it to me several times. Above what number will I be taken seriously? Five? Six? Don't be too greedy to start with, I tell myself; if I say too high a number and they refuse me medication now, I won't have anywhere to go next. Are all my fellow patients running the same calculations? Are they also doing their best to manipulate the more recalcitrant nurses? It's no easy task, using this damned scale to evaluate the intensity of a body's agony. Do we have to put a number on this too? I rebel inwardly, I completely lose my temper once or twice, but with time and my repeated failure to get what I want, I have to accept the situation. The effort is pointless. Questioning the scale, the values, the half-baked numbers—or attempting to explain what I'm feeling accurately: there's no point. When you're in the hospital and you feel like death, and you want something to ease the pain, say nine. Perhaps even nine and a half. You have to go with the scale, take part in its logic; you have to go with the norm and pretend to accept it if you want your own way.

Looking back on it now, the inadequacy of the scale is of a piece with its very enforcement: there is something surreal about having to go through such a rational and codified measure in order to be given a drug that, in the best scenario, will send you off to unchartable wilds, beyond anyone's control.

•

I am at my childhood home, at La Pierre. I'm coming down from the horses' paddock, below the chestnut grove. Farther down, behind the house, there is this place we used to call "the bird garden."

It was called this because before I was born, when my sister Maud was little, our father had put up a big aviary there with dozens of turtledoves. My sister used to love them more than anything—until the day a fox came. It dug a tunnel under and carried out a massacre in there. It killed the lot in one go, and only ate one bird—just one. Maud was crazy with grief. The next day our father took the aviary down; we'll not have any more cages, it's not right, he said; the birds in this garden will be free birds or none at all. So here I am, just above the bird garden as it used to be, the old well in the middle, the little hut on the left with its broken windows, the washing line and the tomtits perched along it on the right, our mother's hazelnut trees and the red currant bushes set all around them. I bend to go under the bar to the horses' paddock, which comes next; I'm on my way to the bird garden. I stop short. Something is coming out of the well: a head. My stomach clenches with fear. Now it is fully visible, as it wriggles clear of the ground. It is huge, light brown, wild. I look away. There's another of them, sitting on the small round stone table. Growling. A third one is coming out of the hut. The one from the well notices me and starts to move calmly towards me. I begin to run but I am so slow—I can't stand that, the slowed motion that happens in dreams, that weighs limbs down just when you need to escape. I slip past them; I'm aiming for the glass door at the back of the house, it looks like they're going to catch me. I run and crawl; I have to use my hands and grip the ground like a quadruped as I try to increase my pace; I'm nearly at the door, I practically scale the ground horizontally, and with a final effort I plunge inside and slam the door behind me.

The therapist looks at me thoughtfully. That was less awful than I was expecting, she admits. Of course. No dream could outdo my actual life. What do you make of it? I ask. She blinks. That bears fill your memories, they roam through your mind, they emerge from your past and...what can I add? Nothing, I say. That's plenty.

•

I've been back at my mother's a few days now. There are bandages around my face and my leg; two very kind nurses take turns checking on me daily. The main thing is the yellow liquid that keeps oozing from under my right jawbone. This is normal, they'd warned me at the Salpêtrière, it will go on for a few days more. But it's been several weeks now. It doesn't really hurt. I'm just afraid, afraid of everything that's still open and unhealed in me, of everything that has found a way into my body. There are other beings lying in wait in my memory; maybe there are also some under my skin, in my bones. This thought is terrifying, because I do not want to be an occupied territory. I want to close my borders, throw out the intruders, fend off the invasion. But perhaps I'm already under siege. It's the same every time. I sink in the face of these thoughts: I know that before closing my borders, I ought to have foreseen a way to rebuild them.

Since I am living with my mother in Grenoble, after leaving the Salpêtrière, I'm advised to go for a checkup at the local hospital's maxillofacial department. I cannot stand this hospital, La Tronche;

45

the mere sight of it makes me nauseous. Someone was very ill here when I was little, perhaps my father before he died, I don't remember now. I make my way across the big square to the Belledonne entrance, at the teaching hospital. I remember the last time I left by this door I vomited on the pavement, right in front of the wrought-iron staircase. I was seven, and our family doctor had diagnosed appendicitis. Later on, in one of the wards, I was told actually that wasn't it. My mother and I had left, relieved, but I only made it a few meters before doubling over, clutching my stomach. I have no wish to be here, I think, stopping for a moment before the great glass doors. I go in anyway. The smell, the linoleum, the colors, the uniforms, the tickets for the queue at reception, all of it repels me.

The results of analysis of my jawbone's yellow ooze are alarming: the surgeon here announces that I've contracted a hospital-borne infection during the Russian plate's replacement with a French one at the Salpêtrière. A resistant strain of streptococcus, known to frequent the Parisian operating table, has made itself at home on the new plate that was meant to save me from the poor quality of its Russian rival. Worse, it is reproducing fast and is in the process of colonizing the whole structure. They are concerned for the bone in my jaw, concerned that it's next in line for colonization. And then, madame, they say, then it will be much harder to get rid of; the bug could spread, could travel all over your body. My fears are coming true: I am actually being invaded. I might have enjoyed the irony had I not been so demoralized by this revelation, and alarmed by the implications. The La Tronche surgeon will brook no discussion. For her, the situation is clear. Once again the Salpêtrière's practitioners have demonstrated their incompetence. I'd grown used to the idea of my jawbone as the theater of a Franco-Russian cold war, but I was not expecting to play host to a competition between French hospital authorities, namely, the petty rivalry between Paris hospitals (hereabouts known as "the factories") and the provincial ones, considered to operate on a more human scale (you're not a number here, you're a person, etc.).

The La Tronche surgeon likewise confirms that the whole job will have to be redone. She outlines her plan: in order to do things properly this time, she will go in again, remove the infected plate, clean out the whole cavity, and replace the internal brace with an external armature system. At that moment I drop to the very depths of the chasm into which I first sank at the clinic in Klyuchi. I picture myself with screws sticking out of my face and a metal jaw screwed onto it; I see myself mechanized, robotified, dehumanized. Tears pour down my cheeks, I stand up. No, I say, just that: No you will not do that. And I leave the room. Wait! Come back! I run down the corridor. Get out of this cursed hospital, that's all I can think of, I sprint down the steps two at a time, white green white green; I need to think, find a solution, some peace, some peace.

It was the physiotherapist in Grenoble who I used to see for lymphatic drainage sessions who sent me to this surgeon for my tests—

47

she's a friend of mine, really knows her stuff, my physiotherapist had assured me. Instead of protecting myself and canceling appointments so I can think in peace, I compound my errors and show up for the massage session booked for the next day. Warned by her bosom colleague, who has told her my test results as well as relayed my violent reaction to the surgeon's plan, the therapist turns into my worst nightmare. While her rubber-gloved hands align over my face to direct the flow of lymph away, she reminds me how serious nosocomial infections can be, the risks I run by not following the surgeon's recommendations, for she "knows better" than I the most appropriate course to take. Her hands come and go. She presses her case home: if I don't do exactly as I am told, it could have far-reaching effects; I might even end up like poor Guillaume Depardieu after his accident; I might even commit suicide. Her gloved hands lift; the session is over.

Leaving the therapy center, I raise an exhausted face to the white sun. Did I need that? Once again I will have to look deeply into myself. I think of the bear. If he's alive, at least he is living his bear life free from attacks like this, symbolic and actual, without paying this price. But who knows? Perhaps the bears also have their processes for casting out their own, their ways of marginalizing "outsiders," of cutting loose those who no longer conform. I lower dazzled eyes, get into the car, engage the car key. No matter. I shall not see these people again.

•

I go back to the Salpêtrière to consult the surgeon who carried out my last operation—the one who, by replacing the Russian plate with her French one, allowed my microscopic invader to take up residence in my jaw. Of course this isn't her fault, but I do blame her, somehow, and I feel that it's up to her to find a solution. She suggests opening it up again to clean it all out, and then taking some of my pelvic bone for a bone graft. And one thing more: they'll have to extract a tooth, a molar, to leave nothing to chance and avoid any fresh infection. Think it over, she says. And this is what I do, for three days, staring at the sea, at my sister Gwendoline's house. I think.

October is almost done. I am sitting at a café terrace in Arcachon. The sea lies in front and the autumn sun behind me, warming my hairless head branded by the animal from another world—the world where there's no strolling on pink paving stones under white streetlamps and palm trees for shade. I look at the boats and their rusty chains vanishing down below the water's surface. I wonder if I would do better to accept my profound mismatch with society, if I should moor myself to my mystery. The boats drift, and I am remembering the searingly intense moments after our skirmish. The self-evidence of the forest, the lucidity that meant I decided not to die. I want to become an anchor. A very heavy anchor that sinks right into the depths of the time before time, the time of myths, of the womb, of genesis. A time close to when humans were painting the "well scene" in the Lascaux caves. A time when the bear and I, my hands in its fur and its teeth on my skin, forge a mutual initiation, a negotiation over which world we are to inhabit. The boats float, and I visualize this anchor disappearing into a space that predates me and that brought me about. I decide that if I berth my vessel here, it will drift no further: it will rock gently on the living surface of the present.

Now I need to decide on closing up the gaping breaches in my body, still holding me in this uneasy liminality—soon, perhaps, to become unlivable. The boats are floating and people are walking on the pink paving. OK. Being me today means refusing consensus, circumventing concord without quite resorting to hara-kiri. OK, I will have another operation.

•

November in Paris, between rain and fog. The bear carried off a bit of my jaw and two of my teeth in its mouth, three months ago. The surgeon is going to pull out a third. A tooth for a tooth. Three. Everything comes in threes. I am lying on the operating table, waiting. Picture a pleasant place, says the nurse who is injecting me with the general anesthetic. This makes me laugh, and my laugh prompts a responding smile on her face. I am thinking that there's no exit out there. I was the one who walked like a wild thing along the spine of the world—and he is the one I found. And I'm the one going through these medical ordeals because there was an "us." There was me and him and no one else in that moment. I close my eyes. The trees appear, volcano in the distance. The fishing boat floats silently on the river beneath the arching foliage. It's summer and it's snowing; it's snowing and it's a miracle.

•

My sight is always blurry when I come round from anesthesia, I can't get used to it. There is this feeling of foreignness that I get every time, like when you've returned from a long journey and you're back home but you no longer feel truly at home there. I am trying to regain possession of this body from which I've been absent for some hours. Was I really there? The memory of my dream is so real. I floated, felt, walked, tasted. I spoke to the one I'm not meant to understand. I told him we could make peace. My vision is clearing: I am indeed back in this odorless yellowed room. Though there is something: it smells of alcohol. Or medicine. I feel sick. I am still alive. I gently touch my face and throat. Something is missing. On the left side of my neck, since the first, failed, French operation, I've had a ganglion. A ganglion growing there in reaction to the nosocomial microbe formerly resident on the now extremely clean titanium plate implanted in my jaw. I have just left recovery and returned to my hospital room, and I'm worried. I ask the junior doctors what happened to it. They were meant to sample a section of the ganglion for analysis. This is not what happened: in the heat of the moment, and in order not to be held up by a "trifle," they quite simply decided to remove it. Ablation is much simpler, they say. Some skin, my hair, three teeth, a bit of bone, and now a ganglion. The list of my body parts lost in battle is growing.

•

Once more I'm alone in the room, and in pain. A few hours ago I vomited blood. I am at 9.9 on the scale no question, and it's plain to see; morphine comes to save me from complete collapse. The ceiling lights dim, a sweet warmth flows through my skin while the pain fades, and I settle more comfortably. I open my black book and I am scribbling right through to sunrise. That night, I write that we need to believe in the wild beings, in their silence, in their restraint; to believe in their watching, in the bare white walls and yellow bedclothes of this hospital room; to believe in the retreat that works upon body and soul in a nonplace that offers neutrality, indifference, and transversality. The formless takes shape, becomes clear, is redefined calmly, abruptly. De-innervate reinnervate combine fuse graft. My body after the bear after its claws, my body bloodied, reborn of death, my body filled with life, with threads and hands, my body as a wide-open world where multiple lives meet, my body repairing itself with them, without them; my body is a revolution.

At the end of the night this appears very clearly to me: I want to thank *her* hands, her woman's hands which had no idea, which were also not expecting to grapple with the ruptures opened by the creature from the other world. Her hands, which picked out, cleaned, replaced, closed up. Her civilized hands, which seek solutions to the problems of wild animals. Her hands, which find their own peace with the memory of a bear in my mouth, which play a part in the adaptation of my already hybrid body. That night I decide we ought to make a place for their healing, a place at the side of all those still roaming beyond the north wind, a place beside all the acrobats, hunters, and dreamers who are so dear to me. I must find that point of equilibrium which permits the coexistence of elements from divergent worlds, laid deep inside my body without negotiation. Everything has already happened: my body has become a place of convergence. It is this iconoclastic truth that must be accepted and digested. I must defuse the animosity between and within these fragments of worlds so that I may consider here only their future alchemy. And in order to complete this mission of body and mind, from now on my immune frontiers must be closed off, the gaps must be stitched, reabsorbed—I mean, I must decide to close up once more. I need to scar. Closing means accepting that everything left inside is now a part of me, but from now on nothing more. I think: it must really look like Noah's ark in there. I close my eyes. The water is rising the piers are flooded we must raise the anchor batten the hatches; we have everyone we need to face the ocean; farewell we're going to sea.

•

This morning the surgeon sweeps in, all smiles. White coat, green shoes. Her lovely long red hair is tied back. How are you feeling? And the classic dialogue that follows. Yes the operation was successful, you will be all right now, yes I have every confidence. I tell her her job is really something and that I thought about her a lot last night. Awkward smile. Well, it's no small thing that happened to you, she says. Are there other survivors or are you the only one? It's the same as for women in your position, I reply: There are some but not many.

I understood something important today. Recovering from this clash is not only an act of self-focused metamorphosis, it is a political act. My body has become a territory where Western surgeons parley with Siberian bears. Or rather, where they try to establish communication. The relationships being spun within the little country my body has become are fragile, delicate. It's a volcanic country, landslides can happen at any moment. Our work, hers and mine, and that of the indefinable thing the bear has left deep in my core, consists from now on of "maintaining the lines of communication."

I propose that surviving the confrontation with the bear, just as much as confronting *what's to come* in this world, means accepting re-creation in the shape of structural transformation. The unity that so fascinates us is finally revealed for what it is: a delusion. The figure is reconstituted following its own unique pattern, but out of elements that are completely exogenous.

•

Two weeks have gone by, the results are satisfactory and I am allowed to leave. I am on the train, it's six in the evening, I'm racing towards the Alps. I think of my mother waiting for me, of my lavender-scented sheets, of the little dishes of pureed food she is already preparing, of her hands in my hair, which is growing back. My phone rings. I turn to the window and answer softly. It's the junior doctor, in a panic: You must return to Paris straightaway. Take great care to speak to no one and approach nobody. The ganglion has just revealed something. I close my eyes, a lead weight comes down on my head. For a fortnight it has given nothing away, that stolen ganglion. Why does it have to show up now, just when I am at last exiting those walls and not fleeing, when I can envisage the shape of a genuine, uncomplicated convalescence? What drove it to resurface from its culturing darkroom out of the blue, to catch me midflight? Worse, why do I detect a kind of sick pleasure in this doctor, dutifully exercising his power to hold the truth over his patient, who is apparently unable to sense the true state of her body? I feel mounting rage. Or despair—I can't tell. The doctor is beside himself, he is shouting into the phone. I'm telling you to get out at the next station and to take a train back the other way, he orders me. We have good reason to suspect tuberculosis.

Tuberculosis? In me? No, I don't think so; I don't feel anything, I tell him. Unfortunately so, madame; I know this is hard for you to hear, but this is how it is: it is urgent that you return. I hang up. As I do every time that I feel hopeless and don't know which way to turn, I call my mother. Who tells me not to change my plan at all, to come straight back to the house. And no, we shall not wear masks; no, we will not quarantine ourselves: for no, you do not have tuberculosis. My mother is an exceptional woman. She studies the planets' alignment. She forbids me to return to Paris or even to give any further response to the hysterical junior doctor ordering me to leave the house in order not to infect my family. My mother makes me dinner. She tells me she loves me.

At the tail end of the evening, my phone suddenly stops vibrating. It is November 13. The following day, the same strange silence, in such contrast with the lunacy of the day before. I turn on the radio and discover why. The attacks at the Stade de France and the Bataclan concert hall in Paris have just happened—France is in a state of grief. The Salpêtrière is overwhelmed, and especially the maxillofacial section. The irony of contingencies: *kairos*. The horror of that massacre is what spirits me out of the doctors' clutches, and they forget about me. I am left to myself and my mother. I can breathe.

•

I spend my days reading and looking out the window, waiting for the night, for its cover, its dreams and visions, the chance to travel. I don't talk much. I want to enjoy this insularity, to build it up in my body even while acknowledging the incommensurability of the creatures that populate my inner island. I tell myself: It's not about depopulating the soul so as to enjoy the insular little strip it still harbors; rather it's about making of ourselves the place, the ecosystem where those we have chosen—or who have chosen us—become, beyond the gulfs that divide them, commensurable. Snow is falling outside, I am the fisherman holding the fish in my arms. The snow settles along the branches, I am the fish cradled in the hunter's arms. The snow covers everything, I am the fish diving back in and turning into a brightly colored bird beneath the river's cold, dark surface.

That night, for the first time in a very long while, I see Dasho. We are at Fort Yukon in Alaska, in the cabin where I lived on my first ethnographic field trip. I am weeping. I tell him it's so hard with these scars. Look at me, he says. I look at his face. I examine it and discover fine lines there, scars I had never noticed before. He rests his hands on my shoulders, tells me to be calm. My tears stop. Remember, he murmurs. The scene changes. We are transported to the top of a cliff overlooking the taiga. It's a weird place; it looks much like the Hautes-Alpes, where I'm living right now, but also like Alaska's Yukon Flats and like the Icha in Kamchatka. We stand there without speaking, listening to the sounds floating up from the forest below. Then he says: You always were made for this land. Silence. He closes his eyes and opens his mouth, a long roar rings out, echoing again and again as it explodes into space.

•

I am lying on the bed; I've just hung up. I was speaking to my therapist, Liliane. I've known her a long time; it was she who helped me when my father died fourteen years ago. I am trying to think about what she's just told me. The bear marks out a boundary. The "bear" event and its sequelae are asking me, once and for all, to let go of the hostility with which I face the world. I try again: in the encounter between the bear and me, in his jaws against my jaws, there is an inexpressible violence, which gives form to the violence I carry with me. If I follow the thread of her thought, it's that I went out in the world looking for something that's inside me; the bear is a mirror; the bear is an expression of something other than himself—of something to do with me. I roll onto my back and stare at the raindrops running down the skylight. I am annoyed. Worse, I'm enraged. It's a smart bit of argument. The word that comes to mind is *clever*. But something rings false, something fundamental that I can't quite grasp yet. I mutter to myself, listening to the rain. I hate this sense of sacrifice that's cropping up everywhere. What is going on here, for all the other souls around us to be reduced to mere reflections of our own states of mind? What are we making of *their* lives, of their trajectories through the world, of their choices? Why in this business, in order to unknot the threads of meaning, must I bring everything back to myself, to my actions, my desires, my death drive? Because what lies deepest in the other's body will remain forever inaccessible to you, I've no doubt Liliane would have replied. Even more so, what lies deepest in a bear. This is true, and it torments me. Who can say what he carries with him, what he feels; who can explain the reasons that prompt his movements, beyond the basic, functionalist explanation? There are things I will never know, this much is obvious. Which does not mean I should give up, renounce the obligation to understand further.

My other problem today is the symbolism: it catches up with me even when I reject it, and it's wearying me profoundly. Thinking about the bear from where I happen to be, in this room in my mother's house in France, I cannot escape the play of analogies. I inevitably wonder what the figure of "the bear" might correspond to here in the West (I already have my own ideas about the animist aspect of the question), what it might reflect. I draw up lists to pass the time; the lists make me laugh even while they depress me.

Strength. Courage. Abstinence. Cosmic and terrestrial cycles. Artemis's favorite beast. The wild. The lair. Retreat. Reflexivity. Refuge. Love. Territoriality. Potency. Motherhood. Authority. Power. Protection. And the list goes on. I have come to a pretty pass.

If the bear is a reflection of myself, which symbolic expression of this idea am I now exploring most assiduously? Were it not for his yellow gaze answering my blue one, I might perhaps have been contented with these correspondences. Although I would prefer to use the term *resonance*. But our bodies *were* commingled, there was that incomprehensible *us*, that *us* which I confusedly sense comes from a very distant place, from a before situated far outside of our limited existences. I turn these ideas over in my head. Why did we choose each other? What truly do I share with this wild creature, and since when? The truth as I see it is that I've never sought to bring peace to my life, far less to my encounters with others. On this point my therapist is correct: I am not at peace. I don't even know what the word means. I've been working for years in a Far North rocked by profound transformations. I know how to work with metamorphoses, explosions, *kairos*, crises. I find things to say, for times of crisis always seem valuable to think through—because they hold the possibility of another life, a new world. On the other hand, I have never known what to do with peacefulness or stability; serenity is not my strong suit. I consider that out there on the high plains, I must subconsciously have been seeking the one who would at last reveal the warrior in me, that this must surely be why I didn't run away when he blocked my path. On the contrary: I plunged into battle like a Fury, and we branded each other's bodies with the sign of the other.

I struggle to explain it, but I know that this encounter was planned. I had marked out the path that would lead me into the bear's mouth, to his kiss, long ago. I think: who knows, perhaps he had too.

I think that, as children, we inherit territories we must go on conquering throughout our lives. As a little girl, I wanted to live because there were wild animals, there were horses and the forest's call; because of the great expanses, the high mountains, and the unbridled sea; because of the acrobats, tightrope walkers, and storytellers. The anti-life consisted of the classroom, mathematics, and the city. Luckily, on the threshold of adulthood, I discovered anthropology. This discipline became an escape route for me as well as the possibility of a future, a place where I could express myself in this world, where I could become myself. I simply had not anticipated the impact of this choice, still less the implications of my work on animism. Without my realizing it, every single line I had written on relations between humans and nonhumans in Alaska had prepared me for this encounter with the bear—had, in some way, prefigured it.

Weary, I feel unable to take this any further for now. Rain is still dripping down the skylight, and I must make up my mind to wait. I remind myself that nothing is ever revealed by a gesture. Or rather: that after the intense moments of my near-death and the sense of clarity and insight I had then, a fog has once more settled over those events and over the rest of my life.

•

I don't have tuberculosis. The analysis is official, and the clinicians at the La Tronche infectious diseases department refute their Parisian colleagues' diagnosis. They call the Salpêtrière on several occasions, but—the final touch to this high farce—the ganglion culture has disappeared and no one there can track it down! I submit to a battery of further examinations—still nothing. Not the least hint of a microbe. I have fended off the invaders—assuming the invaders were not a fiction, dreamed up by otherwise meticulous doctors helplessly entangled in a deadly melodrama. I am inclined towards this latter view, but I will never really know the truth.

It is December now, and I must go back to Paris for my post-op meeting with the surgeon. Packed waiting room, numbered tickets, green seats, green linoleum, hospital smell, overriding desire to vomit, knot of anxiety deep in my guts. At last it's my turn to go in. She is waiting for me: white coat, green shoes, red hair tied back. You're doing well, she says, examining me; no ooze, no infection, and the X-ray shows that the graft has taken and my mandibular bone is growing back. Within a few months, we'll have you chewing and eating solids again. In a few weeks, I'll see you for a follow-up. That, I believe, you won't, I retort, in my head. In a few weeks, I won't be here anymore.

•

I am walking the streets of the Eighteenth Arrondissement, a thick shawl around my neck and face to protect my scars from the drizzle and blustery wind. It's that damp, freezing Parisian chill that creeps right under your skin. I come to rue de Ponthieu and pick out the VHS Russia—Visa Handling Service—building. I go inside and wait, again. I reflect on the likelihood that my plan will succeed. I remember how, in my hospital room in Petropavlovsk, I slyly observed the form that the FSB agent was filling in so conscientiously. I very clearly recall seeing him write *Marten* instead of *Martin* and *Nastasia* instead of *Nastassja*. Good old Cyrillic alphabet with its phonetic equivalents, I had thought. Helpful that he filed me under a different name. But will that be enough? As long as it works, I tell myself again and again, a silent prayer.

My number is called, and I go to the counter. All the documents are present and correct, stamp, payment, nothing to report, I have my visa.

•

Big tears are rolling down my mother's cheeks. I came back from Paris yesterday, and we are at the table, about to have lunch. I don't know how to tell her any less bluntly; delicacy has never been my forte: I'm going back out. When? In two weeks. I'm free of infection, the X-rays are all clear and there's no uncertainty: I can go. I go on to say that living at my place is out of the question for now, that I can't handle my friends' faces when they look at me—the pity in their eyes doesn't help me see beyond what's put right in front of me. I have to get away in order to get well—to be protected from people. From doctors, and their prescriptions and diagnoses. Far from antibiotics and even farther from electric lights. I need shadows, a cave, a refuge, I want candles, nighttime, gentle shaded lights, cold outside and warmth inside, and animal skins to insulate the walls. Maman, I must go back to being *matukha* and retreat into my lair, to spend the winter there and restore my vital energy. Besides, there are mysteries I haven't yet understood. I need to go back to those who know bears and the questions they bring with them, who still speak with them in their dreams, who know that nothing happens by chance and that our life paths always cross for very particular reasons.

My mother weeps, but she knows, at heart, that this is my only option. Later on, most of her friends will undermine her resolve by peddling their tales of personal boundaries again. I encountered the bear because I didn't know how to set boundaries between myself and the outside world; I couldn't set boundaries because my mother couldn't ever set any for me. You should have laid down the law for once and said no to your daughter. You need to rein her in. Make her see reason. Stop her. Restrict her. Poor Maman, poor friends. It's true, I never have responded well to conventions or diktats, and I have appreciated decorum even less. But, darling mother, I'm going this time so you will understand that this thing with me and the bear is not just another instance of insufficient boundaries and projected hostility. My mother stands her ground, she doesn't give way; my mother understands that her daughter has a bond with a forest and that she must vanish back into it to complete her inner healing.

Luckily we have Marielle. Cool, distant, and fair. It's not incidental that Marielle works with the law. Marielle is our closest friend, my mother's and mine. It's strange: Marielle, who never leaves the city, a beautiful woman done up to the nines, perfectly turned out, hair styled, artificial even. It's strange but I think she understands my wild-world problems. When she hears the news of my next stint away, she talks to my mother, talks in her own language, that of celestial bodies and myths, of resonances and correspondences. She reminds her about Artemis and her forest, which she would fall apart without. She talks about Persephone, who returns annually to the underworld in order the better to climb back up into the light. She talks to her of movement and duality, of metamorphosis and masks, of refiguring after a disfigurement, of spring following winter. One day Marielle even makes me cry: touching my red scars she says that now I embody the goddess of the woods.

•

December. I have come back to my own home in the mountains, ahead of my departure. It's snowing. I gaze through the window at the peak of La Meije, which is quietly fading into the mist. I wipe from my mind the eyes of a friend who didn't recognize me at first when we bumped into each other at the garage. Poor thing, was all he said. It's not so bad, I replied, before escaping into the car of my neighbor, a local, who'd come to pick me up. Forget about it, my neighbor said when he saw my tears, and offered me a beer back at the house.

I spend some time reading, and I'm trying to write but not really managing. I take out my field notebooks and the black book. I open that one, flick through the pages. Suddenly I stop, dumbfounded. I've come across a fragment written before my departure for Kamchatka exactly a year earlier. Time stops. Is there no limit to the performative power of words?

DECEMBER 30, 2014

On the eve of falling into another year another life another me
    simply another
I am trembling with fear
The shadow is deep and I am blinded by the night
Prisoner of my unmoving body my knee pinned to the earth head
    bent to the ground
I am waiting
For the beast inside to stand forth again and reclaim her rights
For her to grasp her potency
The days grow longer and the lair is narrowing
The hour to emerge into daylight is near
From the claws that will again dig into the dust a volcano will be
    born
And when the volcano comes alive
The earth itself will tremble.

Snowflakes wheel in the white sky. I think about what the next phase might be. Four months, and the forest there, waiting. The beauty of this thing that happened—happened to me—is that I know everything without knowing anything anymore. Will I feel the birds' feet as they strike the ground again? The rustling of their wings in the distance, the texture of their breath?

Something is happening
Something is coming
Something is descending on me
I am not afraid

Spring

IT IS JANUARY 2. The plane's wheels screech on contact with the frozen ground. I land on the tarmac with the other passengers; it is minus thirty. Yulia and the children are waiting for me at the gate. Yulia does not live in the forest with her family, she only spends four months of the year there, in the summer. Ten years ago she married Yaroslav, a Russian serviceman of Ukrainian extraction. Since then she has lived with him and their children at Vilyuchinsk, the biggest of Kamchatka's naval bases, lying south of Petropavlovsk. Vilyuchinsk is closed to Russian civilians without special authorization; it is off bounds to foreigners full stop, with or without authorization. But Yulia is my friend, my sister, my Yulieta, and simply the only person I want to be with in this rough town. Rather than any cheap, dingy hotel, or indeed any pricey and superficially luxurious one with cardboard-cutout facade and decor, I would a thousand times over choose to follow my friend into her own prison, on the far side of the fjord below the volcano.

We cross the first forty kilometers between us and the base; I can already make out the buildings along the shore, their backs up against the volcano. The checkpoint is not far now: we stop the car in a dip in the road before reaching it. We take the water barrels and blankets out of the trunk. I lie down, fitting myself entirely into the footwell between the back and front seats. Yulia and Yaroslav cover me with the blankets and heap the water barrels higgledy-piggledy on top. I am invisible. My next five minutes are extremely uncomfortable, but after all that's happened to me over the last few months, this feels like a walk in the park. Or at least the accomplishment of a mere formality. I hear the soldier's voice, then that of Yulia's husband answering. I hear his leather boots—black, as I imagine them—ringing on the asphalt. The lid lifts above me and he checks our load. Everything is in order. *Khorosho, do svidaniya.* We set off again. A feeling of walking into the lion's mouth—but it's a new kind of lion, more bloody-minded than your standard big cat, when it gets hold of you. On the bright side: no one will ever find me here, I think. In among all the submarines salvaged from the Cold War and the uniformed army boys, naturally I am well hidden. This is the whole strategy Yulia and I dreamed up, contrary young women that we are: to hide me precisely here, at the danger's source, in my enemy's own bedchamber. You go far enough to sense it inside you, you feel it, you are contained by it and you contain it; if you are strong enough, you will bridle it, you break it. Then, one day, when you have fully understood its ways, you cut yourself loose.

I have poked my head out of the blankets, and the water barrels have gone rolling in all directions. We laugh uproariously. Even Yaroslav can't help bursting out laughing. Transgressing the rules is bringing us closer. Yaroslav turns and fixes my eyes with his blue stare. Shit, so you're the Frenchwoman who frightened off a bear. If we three can't give a soldier the runaround, what hope is left for the world? Our raucous combined laughter has the car swaying on the spot. Then, wiping tears of mirth from her eyes, Yulia sets a finger to her lips and makes an attempt at a straight face. Don't forget, Nastya. Not a word when you're outside. And keep completely shtum in the shops. Your French accent might be recognized. If you keep quiet, no one will suspect you're not Russian.

Shut up. Shun it. Pen it—why not. All is permitted, when you are rising from your own ashes.

•

Through the window you can see the military port with its submarines under repair and navy officers busying themselves among the rusty machines beached all around them. This stretch of the sea is frozen solid. The air is glacial, particles of frost glitter in the winter light, pinkish above the sea, violet over the volcano opposite. It's very hot in the house. So hot we have to open the window to breathe. The temperature can't be adjusted. That's how it is, Nastya, in Russian towns in winter, Yulia tells me.

The apartment consists of two rooms and a kitchen. There's a faded brown tapestry with red flowers. A hip bath in the little bathroom. Damp patches staining the partition walls from top to bottom. Electric wires running everywhere. Cracks zigzagging across walls and ceiling. The tiny kitchen forms the heart of this world. It harbors a little table with a beige plastic cover, also flowers, four stools, a gas stove, a sink, and a tiny window that looks out the back of the building, where a great heap of snow, several meters high, forms the view.

69

Here we sit for a good part of the night, Yulia and I, telling women's stories and talking politics. We drink our vodka slowly but surely, a little glassful an hour. She shows me her photos of the forest. Here is my mother gutting the fish; this is Ivan fishing; here's Volodya looking after the horses. Ah, and here are you and Mother having tea two years ago, do you remember? Yes, of course I remember, my Yulia, remembering is my business. At some point in the night when we are out of words and vodka, I lie down to sleep in the bed beside Vassilina, her daughter. She likes it when we share the bed; I do too. When we wake we stay under the covers for a while, whispering. She pats my short hair, it makes her laugh, it's different, she says, but it's funny. She starts telling me about the forest and Tvayan. She wonders what they're up to right now. Look it's ten o'clock. Perhaps babushka is cooking. Perhaps Ivan is coming back from hunting. Or perhaps they have gone to find wood. Perhaps they must have.

Later that day Vassilina does some drawing. She draws trees, the river, foxes, the house in Tvayan, fish. She draws the shapes of all her absent family and tirelessly colors them in. I like drawing, because this way I get out of here, she explains. Papa says I mustn't dream too much. What do you say about dreaming? I consider. I think that we shouldn't run away from whatever remains unfinished deep inside us, that we have to confront it. I don't know how to translate that into simple words, so I say: Vassilina, if growing up means seeing your dreams die, then growing up becomes dying. It's better to ignore adults when they try to tell us that the boxes are already there, just waiting for us to write the answers in.

70

•

I leave that morning. One of Yaroslav's friends is driving, much too fast for my liking, a green and rusty 4x4. I don't like this Kolya. His sagging cheeks are flushed, and sweat drips down his forehead. I had no choice: he was the only person Yulia and Yaroslav knew who could be free at such short notice, and he's agreed to take me to the edge of the forest over eight hundred kilometers away, for a modest sum negotiated on the fly. We stop at Mil'kovo to stock up on water, gas, and food. It's already dark. A row of crumbling concrete blocks. Yuri Gagarin on one facade, CCCP, the star, hammer and sickle: we are so close to leaving all this behind. In Mil'kovo, as everywhere in Russia's Far East, this past was barely yesterday. Inside the shop, I pull my fleece snood as high over my face as I can, but fail to hide my swollen right jaw. The cashier stares: Do you have toothache? Yeah, that's right. I have toothache. Keep it together. We dive back into the car.

The 4x4 jolts along the frozen surface. Eight hours rattling through the glacial cold. A light at the end of the road: Sanush', at last. I can see headlights. A snowmobile is parked at the roadside. Relief. I extricate myself from the seat. My face hurts, my head too, everything hurts. I can see him waiting for me in the darkness: Ivan. I fall into his arms, I can hardly stop the tears, I want to tell him everything right now, how hard it's been, how I almost died there, how alone I've felt with the bear-marks all over me. But I say nothing, because they are watching us—they, the two Russians at the

71

Sanush' checkpoint, guarding the nickel mine. They smoke and watch us intently from the door of their yellow hut. They patently have no idea what they're seeing. Two strangers with nothing in common embracing as if they're family.

I need to prepare for the cold we'll be traveling into. I go up to the guards' hut at the checkpoint and approach the two men. From this perspective, it's like a reassuring beacon in the midst of frozen lands. A fine optical illusion, I think; since the previous guard Alexei went, there's nothing left of the refuge, the welcoming lantern that Sanush' used to be, in the depths of the night. Sanush' is a no-man's-land between two worlds; it is another Styx with its own Cerberus.

I say hello, how are you, and ask to go inside in order to change my clothes in the warmth. At last one of the Russians recognizes me. Nastya, is that you? Well, yes. The same infuriating stare. Inside, I take off my wool hat, pull on a balaclava and, over it, the deerskin *chapka* that Ivan's mother, Daria, sewed for me. This guy—I don't remember his name because he's another I've never liked—he clocks my short, almost brown hair. He looks me up and down while he smokes. What happened to your pretty blond hair? Bastard. I take it on the chin. What a shame, he goes on. Yeah, I reply laconically. Then he starts mouthing off about the indigenous people who live somewhere in the forest beyond the mountains, so poor and hopeless they haven't even got houses or electricity; they must surely be living under roots or in hollow trees like animals, he goes on. He is showing his disgust at seeing me go back there. I stop listening. While I finish sorting myself out, my thoughts turn to the great white dog called Shaman who protected Charles and me from the bear right here a few years ago, the big white dog with gentle eyes which that thug killed one night in a drunken spree. Poor Shaman. Poor Alexei. If he knew, he'd be mad with grief. Get out of here fast, I think.

A squall of wind and snow floods into the room when Ivan opens the door; be quick, we've a ways to go and it's late. The two men glare at each other for a moment, wordlessly, and silence falls on Sanush'. I gather up my things, minimal leave-taking, and I am outside. I settle on the skins in the snow sled, pull on the mittens, and grip the ropes tightly. The motor growls. The stark light disappears behind us, the night's darkness thickens. We are swinging into the forest. I close my eyes and let the cold numb me, I breathe.

My chains remain lying there in front of the hut in Sanush', at the feet of those two goons; my limbs are untied, free to move at last. Tears start to flow and then flood down my face and freeze on my skin. The feeling of leaving the world behind me—a version of the world—my world, where I can't function any longer, where I keep failing to understand myself.

•

Three years ago Daria described the fall of the Soviet Union to me. She said, Nastya, one day the light went out and the spirits came back. And we returned to the forest. On my sled in the icy darkness, I allow my thoughts to linger on that phrase. Where I live, the light has never gone out and the spirits have fled. More than anything, I want to turn the lights out. Tonight I too am returning to the forest.

73

•

It is midnight and we are coming into Manash', the first hunting camp of the Even family I lived with for all those years. Ivan's uncles are waiting for us. We drink tea in silence. It's good, you stayed alive, Artyom says at last. You mustn't be angry with him. You know how they are . . . They are like us. I know, I reply. I don't really feel like talking; he knows, he feels it, and he says no more, and goes to bed. Tomorrow you'll be a new person.

At dawn, I look out through the cabin's little window and see a Buran sitting not far away, among the trees, its orange bodywork faded almost white and engine uncovered. What's that, I ask Ivan, giggling. That's her, he replies, teasing me: Our ride the rest of the way to Tvayan. Yesterday's sled belongs to Artyom. That one's mine. Ah. And will she go? I'm doubtful. Of course she will! We pile our provisions onto the snowmobile, with my bag on top, and I get on. As usual, Ivan travels with nothing. We set off. For the whole day we weave noisily between the trees, making our way west, the Ichinsky volcano receding behind us and with it the source of the Icha, which crosses this vast stretch of forest before racing to join the Sea of Okhotsk. We have a good hundred kilometers to cover. We stop now and then to stretch our legs, to revive our feet and to fix the Buran, which regularly overheats or sputters out. Ivan takes off his mittens, gets his hands into the motor, ties ropes and string around loose parts, then pulls his mittens back on. He laughs. You see, nothing's really changed here. The Buran is a bit like a reindeer—you lead her with ropes, too! We go on. In the full face of the wind, the temperature must be around minus fifty. I think of the wooden cabin in the snow, of the fire, of Daria waiting for us. Tvayan truly is one of the ends of the earth.

•

We have been in Tvayan a few days now. I am doing my best to do nothing; ideally I would even stop thinking. This morning, I decide I really need to not want—not want to understand to heal to see to know to foresee—right now. In the heart of these frozen woods, you don't "find" answers: first you learn to suspend your reasoning and allow yourself to be caught up in the rhythm of an existence entirely organized around staying alive in a forest in winter. I'm trying to discover a silence in myself that's as deep as that of the great trees standing outside, unmoving and upright in the cold. I've made a U-turn, a total volte-face. I have gone back over my steps, like the sables confusing their pursuers in the snow. I don't know where I'm going—perhaps nowhere; I'm safe in my lair, and that's enough. I register the vastness all around us and the tiny everyday gestures inside, the expression of a limitless patience peculiar to humans keeping warm while they await the explosion of spring.

Every day Daria minces reindeer meat for me, saves the marrow from the bones, gives me strips of raw liver (for my digestion), raw heart (for healing), and lung meat (for my breathing). She also gave me a cup of the hot blood (for strength) when we killed the reindeer.

75

Between these walls, I am more vulnerable than I have ever been, and this is precisely why I can now *see*: the sober beauty of their daily comings and goings, the necessity of their smallest movements, the discretion they show among themselves and towards me. Eventually I let myself be carried by the dynamic of this daily routine; it feels as though one by one I am undoing the steps that led me into the jaws of the bear.

•

Infants possess something that adults must seek desperately throughout their lives: a refuge. It is the walls of the womb, with all the nutrients daily flowing in, that we sometimes need to rebuild around ourselves. I have a strange feeling that when we come to grief, the world will try to return us to that refuge by some stroke of luck; something from elsewhere recalls us to our inner life by trapping us within some unpromising dead end—which is actually our salvation. Four narrow walls, a little door, and minimal interactions—Victor Hugo in his island exile, composing poems with his face to the sea; Aleksandr Solzhenitsyn in the woods of Vermont writing Russian history anew; Leon Trotsky in various prisons giving death the slip and writing as he went; Malcolm Lowry in his waterfront shack re-creating on paper the noise of the world just outside yet out of sight. Isn't what they accomplished also what I am trying to do, from my forest under my volcano, on the way back from the near-death that lay in wait for me? What is this if not daring to step aside so as to see more clearly, to see the signs that beat through me and herald our time in all its contradiction, its fury, its tragedy, and its impending and absolute *finis*. I have seen the intensely other world of the beast and the fearfully human world of the hospitals. I have lost my place here; I'm looking for somewhere in between, where I could rebuild myself. This retreat should help my soul recover. For they do need to be built, these bridges and doors between the worlds; because giving up will never be part of my language.

•

It is five in the morning. I can hear Daria blowing on the embers to relight the fire. I get up from my bed, still wrapped in a blanket, step over the boys lying on skins on the ground, and sit on the little stool next to her before the stove. We wait in silence; eventually the water begins to simmer. The scalding tea warms our bodies. Then she looks at me and smiles in the semidarkness, a calm, shy smile, full of love. She whispers: Sometimes certain animals will make a gift to humans. When humans have done well, when they have listened carefully throughout their lives, when they haven't sown many bad thoughts. She looks down, sighs gently, looks back at me. The bears give us a gift: You, by leaving you alive.

•

I am sitting in the snow by the Icha and thinking about Daria's words. I don't want this feeling, I want to toss my irritation into the water under the ice. I am confused, because I understand two things in what Daria said. The first moves and touches me deeply, and reminds me of all the reasons for my presence in Tvayan. The second is one I cannot stand, it disgusts me and makes me want to run away yet again.

77

Taking up the idea that touches me, there is indeed something more here than what we, in the West, are inclined to believe. People like Daria know they are not alone as they live, feel, think, and listen in the forest, that other forces are at work around them. There is a potency here that's external to people, an intention unrelated to humanity. We find ourselves in an environment that's "comprehensively socialized because it is constantly traveled," as my old teacher Philippe Descola would have said. He revived the word *animism* to qualify and describe this kind of world; I and others have devoted ourselves wholeheartedly to following his lead. The statement "the bears give us a gift" holds in it the idea that dialogue with animals is possible, even if rarely in any controllable form. There is also a basic sense that we live in a world in which we all observe each other, listen to each other; we remember, give to, and take from one other; there is attention paid every day to lives other than our own; and, ultimately, therein is the reason I became an anthropologist.

Why do you want to live with us? Daria had asked me, a few days after we first met. For all of this, I had replied. Because there are some very ancient ways that have not disappeared, and because they are still current among you. But that's not the whole story, and this is the nub of the problem. Let's turn to the aspect that disgusts me, then. When Daria says that, by returning me safe and sound to the world of humans, the bears gave them a gift, the bear and I once more become an expression of something other than ourselves; the outcome of our encounter speaks to absent participants, speaks *of* people who were not there. I am tying my mind in knots trying to see the water that's flowing beneath the ice, and it's tough because the ice layer is thick. For me, a bear and a woman is too big an event. It's too big not to be instantly assimilated into one system of thought or another; too big not to be co-opted by some particular discourse or at least incorporated into one. The event has to be transformed so it can be made acceptable; it must in its turn be *consumed* and then *digested* in order to make sense. Why? Because *this* is too terrible to imagine, because *this* does not fit the framework of our understanding, nor any framework, even that of the hunters living deep in the forests of Kamchatka.

Since this is how it is, since I will necessarily be forced to fit into others' ideas, like a triangular peg into a round hole or a round peg into a square, in order not to become the circle or the square that I am not, I manage to suspend my own judgement. For it was I he sought; and it was for him that I appeared. It is hard to leave sense unmade. To decide: I do not know everything about this encounter; I shall let the assumed desiderata of the bears' world alone; my gift shall be this uncertainty. What we need, then, is to reflect on the places, creatures, and events that lie in shadow, surrounded by empty space, where we meet the experiential crux that no standard relationship can describe, that we cannot map our way out of. This is our situation right now, the bear's and mine: we have become a focal point that everyone talks about but no one understands. This is precisely why I keep coming up against reductive and even trivializing interpretations, however lovingly meant: because we are facing a semantic void, an off-script leap that challenges and unnerves all categories. Hence the rush on all sides to pin labels to us, to define, confine, and shape the event. Not allowing this uncertainty about the event to remain requires normalizing it so that, whatever the cost, it can be made to fit into the human project. And yet. The bear and I speak of liminality, and even if this is terrifying, no one can change that. Branches crunch behind me, someone is coming. I decide: They can say what they want. I mean to stay in this no-man's-land.

A hand on my shoulder. OK there? Yeah, OK. Ivan sits down beside me in the snow, picks out a cigarette, and lights it. Want one? Why not. We smoke in silence. What were you thinking about? I close my eyes. I can't seem to string two words together despite boiling over with ideas a moment ago. And then, suddenly, it crashes over me. I look down, hide my face in my lap, tears start rolling down my cheeks; soon it's a torrent flooding through me. I feel my bones cracking, my teeth breaking, the vice of that jaw letting go, and—it's horrendous—I taste the blood pouring into my mouth. *Arrrggghhh*, I whimper between sobs. Ivan sighs and wraps his left arm around my shoulders; then, twisting around, takes another cigarette from his right breast pocket. Flame, and smoke. You're going through it again? he asks. Yeah, everything. The whole scene, on a loop. Not nice at all, I reply. I wipe my tears off, pull from his embrace. The flashback is starting to fade behind my eyes, I breathe out noisily. Come, we'll have tea, you're frozen. He tosses his cigarette onto the ice and takes my arm to help me stand; we turn away from the river and go back inside.

•

I've eaten my fill of reindeer meat and I'm feeling all right. It's almost impossibly hot, but it's always like that on winter evenings in the cabins before we sleep—the stove has to be filled to last the night. I am lying in the darkness on a reindeer skin but without blankets, the boys are to my right on the floor on other skins, and Daria is sitting beside me, sewing. Natasha and Vasya, her daughter and son-in-law (who at seventy is far older), have just arrived and are preparing their bed beside the fire. *Polovaya jizn*, Ivan likes to say, chuckling, about this life lived right on the ground: *Sex life*.

I think back over what happened earlier. The murmurings of people settling soothe me. I'm floating half asleep when a veil abruptly lifts. I open my eyes again. I see the animal moving to stand across my path—and watching me block his own path. Everything is in that exchange of looks, which prefigures what is to happen. Seen like this, it's almost obvious. I smile to myself. This much I can concede, I think. The wild creature bit my jaw: it was my turn to speak. At this thought, sleep takes me.

Horses are galloping in the snow. There are many of them, maybe a hundred. I'm alone in the middle of the tundra. They charge towards me, a cloud of snow rises, and I am blinded. I close my eyes, prepare for the impact. It does not come; I feel their breath pass to the right and left, again and again, then it's over. I turn around. The white cloud dwindles and disappears.

I open my eyes. The boys' breathing is constant. It is still dark. Daria is lying next to me, eyes open, watching. You were dreaming, she whispers. Yes. What did you see this time? Horses, hundreds of horses in the snow. Good, she says. Horses are always a good sign.

81

They aren't far away, they're speaking to you. They didn't say anything, I reply. They don't speak with words, because you wouldn't have understood. If you saw them, then they are speaking to you.

•

I think of Clarence, the old Gwich'in wise man from Fort Yukon in Alaska, my friend and valued interlocutor for all the years I lived in his village. I always found it amusing when he used to tell me that everything was always "recorded" and that the forest was "informed." "Everything is being recorded all the time," he used to repeat. The trees, the animals, and the rivers: every aspect of the world remembers all we do and all we say, and even, sometimes, what we dream and think. This is why we should take great care with the thoughts we formulate, for the world forgets nothing, and each of the elements within it sees, hears, and knows what has happened, what is occurring now and what lies ahead. There is a watch kept by all living things apart from humans, and their lives are ever ready to spill beyond our human expectations. So every thought-form that we send out goes to join and mingle with the old stories that shape the world around us, as well as the conditions of those who inhabit it.

According to Clarence, there is a boundless realm that occasionally shows at the surface of the present, a dream time which absorbs every new fragment of history as we go on creating them. The world harbors a latency and a volatility, somewhat like the lava waiting beneath the volcano for something to force it out at the crater. This is the reason why at dawn Daria and Vasya lower their voices and whisper in the sleepy yurt as they recount their dreams. Are you afraid of waking the others? I ask one morning. No, I don't want them outside to hear us, Daria replies.

•

With the forest, dreaming is not much fun. I thought it would ease off after the bear, perhaps even that it would stop. I hoped so. To spend dark, empty nights simply asleep, not to keep waking up soaked in sweat before dawn, flooded with images that make no sense in the morning, having to spend all day trying to tease out the meaning. But it goes on. Oh well.

It's not that I don't understand what's happening—what happened to me. I've spent nine years working among those who "go to dream farther away," as Clarence would put it. What are you doing with your tent on your back? I asked him five years ago, on finding him outside Fort Yukon surreptitiously heading for the forest. I can't hear anything here. I can't see anything either. Too much chitchat, too much comfort, too much family, and not enough of anything else. *Too much fuss!* I am off to dream farther away. Right, I take note. With time, I too began to dream up there, but just a little. A wolf that I chase after among the spruces, a beaver that dives beneath the little mounds of ice on the Yukon River and invites me to follow. Nothing alarming, then; I decided these were merely the perceptible signs of that essential empathy which forms my bedrock as a professional anthropologist.

Only when I joined the Evens of Icha, under the volcano, did everything change, or rather, everything intensified then, grew

83

denser. I started to dream all the time. Daria was not alarmed: like Clarence when I was among the Gwich'in, she said this was quite normal, that I should be dreaming in her house. In order to dream you have to have moved somewhere new, she told me one day. This is why I never stay home for too long, she went on. You are so, so far from your house . . . No surprise that you're seeing all these things, she concluded. Very well, I thought, at first; this will make nice material to write about, to get into animism as applied to dreams, the interpermeability of two souls, the tanglement of ontologies, the dialogue between worlds, the transversality of dream-visions, and the rest of it.

What presumption! To think that my inner disturbance would not *genuinely* propel me beyond myself. Unhoused, uneasy, I therefore dreamed. Out of the daily round, apart from my family, outside, as Daria and Clarence had recommended, in order to establish a link with the world beyond—an effective link, I mean. But where, towards what or whom, to direct my listening?

•

I am lying on the belly of a bear; he's holding me with a protective paw. He is big and gray. We talk of this and that, we speak the same language. The bear's body and mine are vaguely merging, my skin mingles with his thick fur. We chat tranquilly, but then I get a dim thump of panic when a second and now a third bear arrive in our bedroom (we are lying on a bed in an unfamiliar house). One is black, the other brown. They are younger, smaller too; they brush against me and suddenly I am in danger; I notice their claws, their teeth, and their disquiet, which now begins to resonate with my own. I can no longer be sure of this encounter's outcome; I am terrified.

I *saw* that dream before the bear, in Tvayan. Daria says that nocturnal visions are not always purely our own projections—as with dream-memories or dream-desires. There are other dreams, like this one, and like the one with the horses the other night, that we cannot control but that we hope for, because they establish a connection with the creatures outside and open the possibility of dialogue. Why is this important? Because these dreams allow humans to choose their paths through each day, and because they give an indication of the tone of the relationships still to come. To dream with a being is to be informed. This is why we actively look out for people returning from a long journey, a long hunt, or some long sojourn elsewhere; this is why Daria is watching me during the night, studying the signs—shivering, sudden movements, whimpers, sweating—that my sleeping body cannot hide.

•

This morning, just as I'm surfacing from the night and the dreams, Daria drags me outside. Come and set a trap in the forest with me, far from the boys, she says. OK. Daria is a true warrior. In Tvayan the old idea that the men do the hunting and the women cook is a complete red herring, a pretty fiction concocted by Westerners proud of their advanced social-role divisions. In Tvayan, they have moved beyond designated sex roles. Here everyone does everything. Hunting, fishing, cooking, washing, setting traps, collecting water, picking berries, chopping wood, and making fires. In order to pursue daily life in the forest, fluidity of roles is essential; the ceaseless movement of all involved, their daily nomadism, means that you must be ready to do anything at any time, for physical survival depends on the collective skills of all those who remain, even when any particular family member is absent.

We plunge through the deep snow; we haven't even thought of our skis, being too focused on slipping out quickly. We cross a branch of the river. There are only narrow gaps between the young silver birches growing densely along the shore; we thread our way among them to reach the cover of the taller trees. We go on with difficulty until at last Daria stops, looks up at the crown of the great tree standing in our way, and smiles. She shows me a hole in the trunk. Here, she says. We brush snow away from around the tree, and I take the rusty iron trap from my backpack and hold it out to her. She positions it, places the salmon tail in it for bait, and sets the spring. *Vot*, it's done. Shall we sit down? We sit. Daria faces me, her eyes on mine. Nastya, she begins. I already told you you were dreaming a lot before the bear. You see, it hasn't stopped. So canny, I think. I am caught, like a rat, trapped before the sable gets a look-in. She goes on: Not everyone can do it. You were already *matukha* before the bear; now you are *medka*, half and half. Do you know what that means? It means your dreams are the bear's dreams as well as your own. You must not leave us again. You must stay here, because we need you.

We retrace our route in the snow. The sable will likely jump on that tree, then onto that one. And then it will surely go around it on the ground, there, and see the fish, Daria says. *Vidno budet*, we'll see. We'll have to check in two days' time—see if someone has fallen into the trap. I laugh softly behind her, shaking my head, letting my feet follow in her steps. Someone has already fallen into the trap and you know it, I think to myself. I should have been expecting this, it had to happen. The question was really just when. Here we are now, I think. I wonder what's to be done now; I am annoyed once again. All I know is that it was these same dreams that drove me out of here six months ago, the same dreams that led me into the bear's mouth. I have no wish to start all that again. I am so afraid of dreaming *with*, again.

•

"Freeing up the past of its repetition a little, this is the strange task to be performed. Freeing ourselves not of the existence of the past but from its ties: this is the strange, sorry task to be performed. Loosening a little the ties of what is past, the ties of what has passed, of what is passing: this is the simple task." I began reading Pascal Quignard ten years ago, when I was in the field in Alaska. Let's just say that this fragment had not then assumed its full resonance.

That my world had been drastically altered before my encounter is undeniable. An alteration of the relationship to the world—this is how academics define madness. How is it manifested? By a period of time, a moment, short or long, during which the borders between ourselves and the outside world dissolve, little by little, as if we were gradually disintegrating and sinking into the depths of oneiric time where nothing is settled, where the boundaries between living beings are still in flux and everything is still possible.

The first thing to disentangle, before the whys behind my escape from the forest that summer, is the how of my escape from my own world and into the forest a few years earlier. A rather superficial thought has been going round my head for some time: no one listened to Antonin Artaud, but he was right. We have to get out of the insanity our civilization is creating. But drugs, alcohol, depression, and *in fine* madness and/or death are no solution; we must find something else. This is what I sought in the forests of the Far North, and only partially found, and it is what I'm still chasing now.

I am a doctor of anthropology, sanctioned by the hallowed seats of learning. I have a partner who lives from peak to peak, a home nestled in the mountains, and a book in production. It looks as though everything is fine. And yet something is gnawing at me, there's something nibbling away deep in my belly, and my head is burning; it's as if I'm coming to an end, the end of a cycle too, perhaps. Meaning is withering, I feel as though I'm living inwardly what I described finding in Alaska among the Gwich'in: I don't recognize myself anymore. It's an appalling feeling, because what's happening to me is precisely what I thought I had observed among those I was studying. The forms I've known as mine are falling away. My writing is foundering, I've nothing interesting to say anymore, nothing worth trying to say. My love has finally seeped away, despite the words, despite the heights, despite the peaks—their demands and their indifference. I am exhausting myself in useless mental convolutions and compensating with physical challenges, but there's nothing to be done, I am going under.

How many psychologists would call me insane if I told them I was affected by things going on outside myself? That the acceleration of the disaster has me petrified? That it feels as though I've lost my grip on everything? So that's what's driving you to hole up in the mountains! Yes indeed, and now you're really losing the plot, because even the mountains are coming apart. Losing cohesion because of melting ice, because of these heat waves. The handholds are crumbling, rocks are falling, this is how it is. And friends are crashing at the foot of the sheer rock face. Am I just spinning out some terrible mountaineering metaphor? I don't think so. I can't define it precisely, but I do have one certainty: something inside me is ringing in response, something that hurts and unbalances me.

It would have been so simple if my personal unhappiness could be summed up by an unresolved family issue: by my father's too-early death, by my not living up to my mother's expectations. Then I could "solve" my depression. But no. My problem is that my problem isn't mine alone. The misery my body is expressing comes from the world. I do believe it's possible to become "not I, but the wind that blows through me," as Lowry said, quoting D. H. Lawrence. And it is common not to make it back after that, as Lowry didn't, and as so many others didn't. I went to join the Evens of Icha, and I lived in the forest with them for a reason far removed from any requirement of comparative research. I learned one thing: no matter how it appears, the world is collapsing simultaneously everywhere. The only difference is that in Tvayan, they live knowingly amid the wreckage.

•

Every morning I dip the bucket into the water hole in the Tvayan river. I stop for a few minutes. I like to watch how the water flows beneath the ice. This hole, fifty centimeters in diameter, is like a window, a skylight. An aperture over the world below, where everything is still moving, while at the surface everything is still, desperately arrested. Don't rely on what is immediately there to be seen, I think, each time. Look further, look more deeply, for what is hidden.

I concede that there *is* a direction to this world we live in. There is a rhythm. An orientation. From east to west. From winter to spring. From dawn to dusk. From wellspring to the sea. From the womb into the light of day. But sometimes I think of Copernicus. Of the treason he committed so long ago by showing that we are not turning the way we believe we're turning—that the manner of the earth's rotation is not as we perceive it, but the opposite of what we perceive. Does Copernicus's realization have anything to do with the dynamic of the return—with the illogical ascent of creatures back to their birthplaces? The river flows down to the sea, but salmon swim upstream in order to die. Life pushes us out of the belly, but bears go back underground to dream. Wild geese live in the south but come back to fill the Arctic skies beneath which they were born. Humans emerged from the caves and woods to build cities, but some are retracing their steps and once more live in the forest.

I say there is something invisible that impels our lives towards the unexpected.

•

Vasya pours the tea into his bowl and inhales, pleased with himself. He has just brought in three fish, after a week of Daria's teasing him with her prophetic dreams and fruitful fishing trips while he was finishing empty-handed every day. When it won't bite, it won't bite, he would retort, coming in from the river. Natasha is making dumplings with the fish, and the oil sizzles on the stove. The cabin is almost empty in the midafternoon. Ivan has gone grouse hunting, and Volodya to gather firewood. Daria is outside, looking after the dogs. Vasya and I are sitting at the low table. I haven't had a chance to talk to him since his return, and I know he's been waiting all week for this opportunity, it's in his eyes. *Chto, skaji.* What, tell me, I prompt, as he prevaricates, asking me if it still hurts there or not, showing me his own scars that cover his arms, souvenirs from the time when he used to labor for the *sovkhoz*, souvenirs from when they were still using unsafe tractors around here.

Bears are the most intelligent of all the animals, he says. They are like humans, as powerful as us. Did you know? I knew. Do you know why he bit your face, he asks. No, I don't. He points to my eyes. Because of them, he says. And laughs. Vasya is always laughing, from the vantage of all his seventy years, even when he is completely serious. He frowns and goes on. Bears cannot stand to look into the eyes of a human, because they see the reflection of their own soul there. You understand? Not really, no, I reply. Yet it's simple, Nastya. A bear that meets a human's gaze always has to obliterate what he sees there. That's why he'll always attack, if he sees your eyes. You looked him in the eyes, didn't you? Yes. Ah! he exclaims, I knew it! I told the others, but Daria is always silencing me, she doesn't want us to talk about what happened. I smile at him. That's because Daria is a mother—mothers don't like seeing their loved ones hurt. Hmm, he mumbles. We take a sip of tea in silence. The difference between the bears and us is they cannot look directly at each other. Do you see now? Yes I see. Luckily they don't have mirrors, otherwise they'd all go mad! Vasya bursts into crystalline laughter, and I laugh with him.

Over the next few days I ruminate over Vasya's words. I can't help thinking of Jean-Pierre Vernant—of a passage from his *Death in the Eyes*: "In this face-to-face encounter with frontality, man puts himself in a position of symmetry with respect to the god . . . Fascination means that man can no longer detach his gaze and turn his face away from this Power; it means that his eye is lost in the eye of this Power, which looks at him as he looks at it, and that he himself is thrust into the world over which this Power presides." For Vernant, to see the Medusa means to cease to be oneself and to be projected into the world beyond, to become the other. For Vasya, to be the human who sees the bear (or to be the bear who sees the human) is to embody reversibility: it is to describe a face-to-face encounter in which a necessarily radical alterity is actually revealed as the greatest proximity—a space in which the one is the reflection of its double in the other world.

I had already thought of Vernant while working on the question of hunting in Alaska. Of that moment when the *fascinus* takes over a body in order to thrust it into madness or death. But I had got it wrong. In *Les âmes sauvages* (The Savage Souls)* I wrote that death was the most effective way to escape the unlivable *limes*, or frontier, that the encounter between two beings from different worlds implies—to escape the cycle of metamorphoses which is then triggered and from which there can be no return. Except that I am not dead, nor is the bear.

For years I've been writing about edges and margins, about liminality, the frontier zone, the space between worlds: about that very particular place where it is possible to encounter a force that is other,

---

*Nastassja Martin, *Les âmes sauvages: Face à l'Occident, la résistance d'un peuple d'Alaska* (Paris: La Découverte, 2016).

93

where you risk being changed, from which it is difficult to return. I have always thought I mustn't fall for the bait of fascination. The hunter is imbued with the scent of the prey and decked out in its pelt, while the hunter's voice modulates in imitation of the other and, in so doing, enters its world, disguised but still the same person beneath the mask. This is the ruse and this the risk. The entire business then turns on either managing to kill so they can *return*—to themselves and to their people—or, instead, failing: being swallowed up by the other and ceasing to be alive in the world of humans. In Alaska, I wrote these things; in Kamchatka, they happened to me. The irony of comparative work, a cute joke courtesy of the two territories that keep watch over each other from either side of the Bering Strait; the oddness of the confrontation of my mind in America looking at my body in Russia.

I followed my archaic encounter all the way through, but I did come back, for I am not dead. Hybridization took place and yet I am still myself. At least I think so. Something that looks like me, with the features of the animist mask on top: I am inside out. The animist principle in humans *is* the distorted face of the mask. Half man half seal; half man half eagle; half man half wolf. Half woman half bear. The underside of the face, the animals' human core—this is what the bear sees in the eyes of the person whose gaze he should not meet. This is what my bear saw in my eyes: his share of humanity, the face beneath his face.

•

For several days the herders and their reindeer have been grazing a tundra that lies alongside Tvayan. They spend their evenings with

94

us when they can, when it isn't snowing too heavily for them to reach us, when the woodsy smell of their skin makes them dream of washing. Two of them, Pavlic and Chander, are Daria's nephews. I like these two. The third is a cousin of hers, Valyerka. He's another matter. I don't like his silences, nor his way of scrutinizing me when my back is turned, but avoiding my eyes as soon as I look at him. He is evasive, slippery. It's been this way from the start: my presence deeply upsets him. A few years ago, one summer evening when I introduced myself to him, he shot back: Anthropologist, spy, same thing. Don't expect anything from me, you'll not get a word. Proof there's still a war on between the East and the West, I thought. Or memories of a war. Since then I've avoided him as far as possible. But in winter, with the huddling enforced by the cold, it's difficult. One day, I was sure he'd try to hurt me, and so it turned out.

We are sitting on the little stools in the kitchen. Valyerka, Pavlic, and me. A bit of smoked fish on the table, some tea. Pavlic is waiting to use the sauna, which has been heating since the morning. Chander comes in, a towel around his shoulders, steam rising from his hair when he opens the door. Pavlic stands and starts looking all around the cabin for his towel. I follow him, go through the door into the other room, rummage in my bag. Here, take this one if you like, it's clean. He smiles, thanks me, and takes it. He goes back into the kitchen and leans over the table to grab his jacket. Put that down, Valyerka tells him. Pavlic looks at him, taken aback. Put down the towel, his uncle demands again. Why? Pavlic asks. Because it is Nastya's towel. She is *medka*. You know what that means? It means we

95

don't touch her things. He looks down at the table, spears a piece of fish, eats it, and lifts his teacup to his lips, as if nothing were amiss. Pavlic, Chander, and I remain on our feet, frozen, dumbfounded.

Daria comes in carrying the water bucket. She has heard everything. She shoots a furious look at Valyerka. Get out, she says. I won't have this in my house, you can go and eat by yourself in the yurt. Valyerka looks up at her and starts shouting. You know perfectly well it's true. You shouldn't be trusting her either. She'll bring nothing but bad things here. When a *medka* comes back from the other side, we should have nothing to do with them. Daria opens the door and points outside. Go. Nastya is family. You can chew on your worries alone tonight. Valyerka's face goes scarlet; he'd like to say more, but it's clear he can't. Daria is at home and she rules her own turf, she is head of the household. Leaning heavily on the table, he knocks the stool over, snatches his jacket from the hooks, and slams the door behind him. The enraged snowmobile roars and a wave of powder snow rains back over the cabin window.

I wish I could disappear six feet underground. Daria takes my arm: Come. We go into the other room and sit on the reindeer skin, away from the others' eyes. She can no longer put it off, she has to speak. She doesn't want to, but she has no choice now, because this time I'm expecting her to acknowledge it, for her to say something about this name that follows me everywhere and that comes from their world, not mine.

Nastya. Are you listening? I'm listening. Don't take this too hard.

And especially, don't think this is your fault. Valyerka is like so many others, he's afraid. Why? I ask. Because the people who are marked by the bear like you, you're the only ones who have made a direct contact with them. So? So you have a closeness that was already there before, which meant that *it* happened, that *it* could happen. I know this, I say. What then? What difference does that make to Valyerka, to his life? This is what I'm explaining: He's afraid. Around here, we say that *medka* are to be avoided and above all we mustn't touch their things. Why? I find her evasions profoundly irritating. Tell me, please, don't keep anything from me. Because they aren't altogether themselves anymore, you see? Because they carry an element of the bear inside them. Daria sighs. For some, it's more than that. We say that they go on being "hunted" by the bear for the rest of their lives. Hunted in dreams, or hunted for real? I ask. Both, says Daria, staring at her feet. It's a bit like these people are under a spell, you understand? I understand. A tear rolls down my cheek. Daria takes the corner of a sheet and wipes it off. So do you also think that I'm under a spell? If I truly am *medka* and being *medka* means being all of that, why aren't you also keeping away? I don't believe any of it, Daria replies. That's all just stories. Here, we live with all the souls, with those who wander, those who travel, with the living and the dead, the *medka* and the rest. Everyone.

It always ends like that, in frustration. You might almost think that *Never follow a thought through* was the rule. Suspending your thought in order to interrupt your words; staying silent in order to survive.

Daria, why won't you say anything more to me? Anything further, or stronger, or more precise? Because when I talk, things happen.

•

This morning I went back to sit on the bank above the river, which goes on flowing under the ice. I want to go back home, back to the other side of the world. See my mother again. Ivan shows up; it's his specialty, standing in the way of sadness. He always says: We're all about living here, no time for self-pity. Are you still bothered by what Valyerka said yesterday? Yes, a bit. Let it go. What matters is that *you* know. People won't stop doing that: thinking about what other people think. It does no good for anyone. He laughs. And he doesn't like me either. He doesn't like anyone. You know? Yes, I know. But that makes no difference, I say. I'll be going soon.

Ivan sighs, no hint of a smile on his face now. Will you go like you did last time? You should listen to my mother. You'd do better to stay with us. You're safe here. Hmm, I reply. And the bears are all right outside, is that it? Stop, he interrupts. You remember in the hospital at Petropavlovsk, when I asked why you left that summer? You didn't reply. You said: You wouldn't understand. Or something like that. You want to know what I think? If you like, I sigh. My feeling is that you don't even know what's pushing you to go further every time. Perhaps so, I allow. Or perhaps this is part of what's unsayable—or untranslatable. Like it's another language, you see, a thing you can experience but can't explain. A thing that's overwhelming, that overwhelms you. Ivan shakes his head, shakes it as if ridding himself of the sadness he hates to feel within his body. He laughs once more. You're funny. You are too. A thing like the dreams? Yep. Like the dreams.

There is a river with a cascade. A very long waterfall. I lean over to look. In the water at the base, there are rocks lurking; it's like an open mouth full of spiked teeth awaiting its prey. I'm trembling. I lie down on the edge so as to stop trembling and to get a better view, but now I'm so afraid I can hardly get up. Ivan and Volodya join me. Follow us, they say. They each take a running dive. I close my eyes and follow suit. We dive down below the choppy surface, clear of the rocks. I reopen my eyes under the water. It is so transparent the salmon look as if they're swimming in air; then I see the hunter swimming ahead of me. Except it's not a man anymore—it's a brightly colored bird that spins on the spot but swims with all the grace of the fish around it. I look at my hands moving before me. Suddenly there are no arms, just red-and-yellow feathers beating the water.

I remember my first dream here, and I say nothing more to Ivan because I have no more to say. I'm not being tricky, and anyway I wouldn't win at that game with him, he's by far the better hunter. I try to sort it out in my head, at least: this thing that has arisen, this sort of a response in the form of an open question, this thing just short of frustration, and the recurring dreams that made me run away from the forest (and so from its inhabitants), and the place they tried to give me. The place I still do not want, a place somewhere between the shamans who left too soon and the *medka* who came too late.

•

Enough is enough, I decided. I'm off; I have to get out of this system of meanings and connections that are threatening my mental stability. Later I will straighten out all these uncontrollable fragments of experience, I will turn them into facts sufficiently distilled and stripped down to be manipulated and laid out in relation to one another. Later, I'll do my work as an anthropologist. For now I have to cut and run: I'm heading to the mountains. I want air, nothing blocking my sight line; cold, ice, silence, emptiness, and contingency; and above all else, no more destiny and especially no more signs.

And yet. It was in the midst of the glaciers and encircled by volcanoes, far from people, trees, salmon, and rivers, that I found him, or he found me. I am walking on this arid high plateau where I've no particular business to be; I am leaving the glacier, coming down from the volcano; behind me, the smoke shapes a cloudy halo. I think of myself as alone, for all the personal, historical, and social reasons well known to us, and yet I am not. A bear, as disoriented as I, is also strolling about these heights, where he has no more business than I do. He's almost mountaineering, then, it's true; what's he up to here, in this treeless land without berries or fish, when he could be happily deep in his forest fishing for his supper? We stumble upon each other; if the *kairos* must have some essential element, it is this. A rugged part of the terrain hides us from each other, the mist is rising, the wind is blowing the wrong way. When I spot him he is already standing in front of me and he's as surprised as I am. We are two meters apart, there's no escape, neither for him nor me. Daria had said, if you meet a bear, tell it, "I will not touch you, don't you touch me either." Sure, fine, but not just then. He shows me his teeth; he must be afraid. I am frightened too, but as I can't run away, I imitate him. I show him my teeth. And everything moves into fast-forward. We slam into each other, he knocks me off balance my hands are in his fur he bites my face then my head I can feel my bones cracking I think I am dying but I'm not, I'm fully conscious. He lets go, then gets hold of my leg. It's my chance to unhook the ice ax, which has been hanging from my harness since I came down the glacier behind us, I hit him with it, I don't know where, because my eyes are closed, I have nothing left but sensation. He lets go. I open my eyes, I see him take off at a run, limping, see the blood on my makeshift weapon. And there I stay, dizzy and blood-smeared, wondering if I'm going to live, but I am alive, I am more lucid than ever, my brain is going a thousand miles an hour. I think: If I make it through this, life will be different.

On that day, August 25, 2015, the event is not: a bear attacks a French anthropologist somewhere in the mountains of Kamchatka. The event is: a bear and a woman meet and the frontiers between two worlds implode. Not just the physical boundaries between the human and the animal in whom the confrontation open fault lines in their bodies and their minds. This is also when mythical time meets reality; past time joins the present moment; dream meets flesh. The scene unfolds in our time, but it could equally have hap-

pened a thousand years ago. It is just me and the bear in this con-
temporary world that's indifferent to our tiny personal trajectories—
but this is also the archetypal confrontation, the unsteady man with
his erect sex standing face-to-face with the wounded bison in the
Lascaux well. And as in the Lascaux well scene, the incredible event
depicted is dominated by uncertainty about its outcome, although
it is inevitable. But unlike the well scene, what happens to us next
is no mystery, for neither of us dies, for we both return from the
impossibility that has happened.

This is not a thought I want to articulate aloud; I prefer to write it.
Today, sitting on the riverbank in wet snow, I write that there is an
implicit, unspoken law specific to the predators seeking and evading
each other in the depths of the forests and upon the mountain ranges
of this earth. The law is as follows: when they meet, if they meet,
their territories collide, their worlds turn upside down, their usual
paths are altered, and their connection becomes everlasting. There
is a kind of suspension of movement, a holding back, a hiatus, a
dazzlement that grips the two wild creatures caught in this ancient
encounter—the meeting that cannot be prepared, nor avoided, nor
escaped.

Upon leaving that exalted no-man's-land of mountains, glaciers, and
high-altitude plateaus, ultimately less uninhabited than I had imagined, I have very few certainties left. The constancy of beings and

things is beyond me; their organization into comprehensible, established systems escapes me; the possibility of their continuity in time is likewise beyond my grasp. My "facts," the facts I carefully collected and had begun to lay out so as to build a world—the one I'd hoped to share with my contemporaries—are now lying at my feet like so many broken links, to be reordered, later on, quite differently. Why? *Potomu chto nado zhit' dal'she.* Because we have to live further, as everyone says who lives here in the forest, along the river, under the volcano. We have to live after, with, and facing this; only live further away.

•

What does it mean to emerge from the abyss where uncertainty reigns and choose to build new boundaries using brand-new materials salvaged from the depths of your dreams' unvarying darkness? From the very depths of the yawning gob of a being other than yourself?

I think of the little muskrat and the man in the Gwich'in creation myth. I think of the limitless ocean on which they float, undecided, open, unconstrained, fluid. I think of that little muskrat diving right down to the ocean floor, where it is dark as night, where he is blind, where he is frightened, to gather in his claws the lumps of peat they will use, he and the man, to create a firm land on which to walk and mark out their respective territories. And I think of the sickly blind man who is helped by a bird, a loon that climbs on his back and, three times over, dives with him into the dark heart of the lake, so

that he returns transformed, endowed with new sight. I consider all
these stories and all these myths that I and so many other anthro-
pologists have painstakingly transcribed in our monographs on
the peoples we've studied, all those journeys from one world to
another that fuel our scholarly interest, all those people with something special, those shamans whom we pursue the way hunters
trail the animals that fascinate them. I think of all those creatures
that have plunged deep into the dark and uncharted realms of alterity and have returned metamorphosed; able to face "what's coming"
at their own pace, they go on with what's been entrusted to them
under the sea, underground, in the sky, in the lake, in the belly, in
the teeth.

•

The days stretch on in the cold, the nights are never-ending. The
air is frosted, solid. It is time to leave, but we say nothing about the
imminence of the departure. That's how it is in the forest: you never
move on bit by bit, you don't prepare, you go on as if nothing will
ever change until suddenly everything topples. And this is precisely
it: being on guard. Taking advantage of the body's stillness up to the
moment when you must make the leap, always when it is least
expected. You can't ever talk of the parting to come, of the moment
after which nothing can be the same. So you live like this deliberately,
in the illusion of timelessness, fully aware that in a second all you
have known will disintegrate and be reshuffled, here or elsewhere,
will metamorphose and become an ungraspable thing that you can
never assimilate again. This possibility terrifies everyone. Because
everyone in the forest knows about it, and because we are always

expecting it around the next corner, we maintain a tacit agreement not to say it.

I am writing on the porch, facing the open door, and the hillock of snow and the tree behind it, a cup of scalding tea next to me on the bench. The temperature is creeping higher, spring is in the air. Volodya goes by, a book in one hand. He stops and sits beside me, looks over my shoulder. Are you writing about the bear, about yourself, or about us? All three, officer. Volodya laughs and looks over the pages of scribble gathering there. You should call it *War and Peace*! I laugh with him. And you, what are you reading? I ask, pointing to his book. He closes his eyes, lays his hands on his knees, and takes a deep breath. *Each man in his night makes his way towards his light.* He opens his eyes again. Beautiful, don't you think? It is. Victor Hugo, my dear.

This morning the river has burst out of the ice. Just like that, in one go. Without warning, everything began to flow. We ought to go, to hurry before the Buran becomes useless on the wet snow. But no, instead we decide to go fishing. You might think I like it, fishing, after more than ten years' work with hunting and fishing people—on the contrary. Especially in winter. Waiting for hours in the cold. Telling yourself they will bite, even when nothing is happening at all. Sticking at it, even when nothing goes on happening. Why does no one ever talk about this? I wonder, rebelliously, staring at my line floating pathetically between small ice floes. About this numbed waiting, about the near miss that generally crowns our failure. Going home, utterly frozen, sinking waist-deep into the spring snow, tea, more tea. I laugh to myself, I giggle at this absurdity that is, nonetheless, the beating heart of life in the forest.

It's always like that here; nothing ever turns out how you want, it resists. I think of all the times when the shot doesn't fire, when the fish don't bite, when the reindeer won't go on, when the snowmobile misfires. It's the same for everyone. We try to maintain some poise, but we trip, we sink deep, we hobble, we fall and pick ourselves up again. Ivan says that only humans think they do everything well. Only humans attach such importance to how other humans view them. Living in the forest is partly this: being a living thing among so many others, going up and down along with them.

•

Spring days. Days of reindeer slaughter. Days of carnage. The herders will take advantage of the shared journey in the offing to go as far as the village and sell their meat. Ivan left for the yurt yesterday to help them. I went to join him, to see, perhaps out of some sense of professional interest, but more than anything out of poor judgment. What I found was an open-air slaughterhouse. I hadn't considered the effect that not one, not two, but fifty slaughtered reindeer dragged through the snow, decapitated and butchered on a make-shift workbench, would have on me. Ivan is killing, chopping, emptying, slicing, piling up, shifting. His hands are red, the snow is red, tufts of hair lie all over the ground and fly fast and far in the frozen wind. I want to be sick. Ivan cannot say why he preferred this vast butchery to staying home; nothing forced him to come, he's not a herder. Going to help, he had said, simply. But to help with what? There are plenty of others.

Ivan's eyes are glazed, while the blood flows like water. I watch him losing himself amid the very reasons that pushed his family to abandon herding for the State and to become hunters once more. He's no longer himself, he is nothing but a death-dealing force. Ivan goes back to the herd, catches one of them in the lasso, leaps onto her, and plunges his knife into the back of her brain. I see him exhaust himself dragging her through the snow, I see the sweat on his forehead as he cuts off her head, eviscerates her, and hangs the carcass on a hook in a tree. Does he wonder what he's doing here? I suspect that in this moment he has forgotten everything: forgotten who he is, forgotten his family's decision, forgotten why they don't do this anymore. But I could be wrong. Perhaps he knows exactly what he's after in this ferocity that foreshadows my departure. I feel that there is indeed a fury boiling inside us. Half body, half mind, a rage that is endlessly ready to tear apart the fragile unity of our lives.

And I—had I known what I was seeking with the bear? Did I know then who I was awaiting, who it was I saw in my dreams? Did I know why I picked up his tracks everywhere and why I was secretly hoping one day to meet his eyes? Not like that, of course. Not so quickly, not so intensely. Leave, I was saying. Air, ice, cliffs, horizon. And blood joined the list. He caught me unaware even in my anticipation. His kiss? Intimate beyond anything I could have imagined. My eyes fill, and everything blurs: the reindeer heads all over the ground, the headless bodies bleeding out, the men busying themselves all around. Ivan, stop, I can't take it anymore. Is it possible to live without the fury that throbs within each of us and threatens, periodically, to annihilate everything? You must always be certain you can find your way back. Back from the other world, like Persephone. Six months on earth and six months under it—easy. But outside the time of myths, the cycle breaks, because that's how it is, because these are our times, because this is what we must all confront. The two faces of the animist mask ought to stop killing each other and instead create life, create something other than themselves. They ought—no: whatever it takes, they must break away from this deadly reflexive duality.

Ivan looks up at me, sees my tears, and hears my silent plea. Leave the blood, let go of death, let's get out. He takes a cloth from his pocket and wipes his knife. He puts it away in the sheath at his belt. I gotta go, boys, see you tomorrow. We walk back to the yurt through the trees, leaving the bloody tundra behind us. Thanks, he says. No problem, I reply.

I keep putting one foot in front of the other. Getting out of here is all I'm thinking about now. I would like to know what Ivan is thinking. But I don't ask him. Silence can be good, sometimes. I still don't truly know where I'm going or who I am. In the end, perhaps he doesn't either. Ivan is returning from all the blood he had to spill in order to be part of a distant modernity. I am returning from the jaws of a bear. The rest? A mystery.

•

Daria is staying here; she almost never leaves the forest. Everything is ready, the bags are on the sleds, the meat too, the dogs are barking, the wolves answer them in the distance. We are walking up the hill that looks over the camp, catching at branches and roots in order to keep climbing the slope. At the top, a tree stump looks out over Tvayan. Would you roll me one? Sure. We smoke in silence, looking at the others working busily below. They can't see us, but we see them. I like it, Daria says.

So you're going? I'm going. Nothing we can do to keep you? No. What will you do? Write. About what? About you, and us, and what's happening. What is happening? The unthinkable. Daria smiles. You and your words. Tell me more. I laugh. You see? I say. See what a nuisance it is when you leave me in limbo? She chuckles; I know I know, but that is the privilege of old age. Not speaking when you don't want to say too much, not sharing proper plans since they never work out as intended. It's a different story with you. I know you, you'll do your thing anyway, so tell me.

I tell her: Daria, I'm going to do what I know; I'm going to do anthropology. And how is it done, the anthropology? she asks, fixing me with her mischievous eyes. I exhale; you're bothering me with your difficult questions. I look up at the sky, throw down my cigarette, and sigh again. I don't know how it's done, Daria. I know how I do it. Are you listening? I'm listening. I go close, I am gripped, I move away again or I escape. I come back, I grasp, I translate. What comes from others, goes through my body, and then goes who knows where.

Are you sad? I ask her. No, she says, and you know why? Living here you have to wait for the returns. Of the flowers, of the animals that migrate, of the souls who matter. You are one of those. I'll wait for you.

I don't say anything, I am moved. This is my liberation. Uncertainty: a promise of life.

Summer

IN FRONT OF ME, the pile formed by my field notebooks from Kamchatka over the last five years. Green, blue, beige, blue, brown, black right at the bottom. I turn to look through the window; La Meije is lit by the fading glow of sundown. I decide. I topple the pile; I open the black book at the end and flip through the last few pages.

AUGUST 30, 2014

"How can you hide from what is *meant* to be part of you? (The mistake made by modernity.)"

—René Char, *77*

What does it mean to be belated in life?
To know feel want always too late
To desire upstream of the world
Those who are absent those who resist those who hold on to
The forests the mountains in their eyes
To be trussed to their freedom to their insubordination
To be held by the impossible
By what should not take place
These encounters that endanger
The institution of the collective its solidity

These links in the form of potentials
Which confer on the explosion on the fragmentation

Wild beings frozen dazzled petrified
Wild things with incalculable trajectories
Wild beings which beset the void
Because their future is merging with nightfall
And because this may be all there is

Wild beings that tender their submission that cease to want
Wild beings that brandish weapons.

Pensive, I close the notebook. I put it away carefully on the shelf and allow myself to smile. I imagine that, since the bear, the black book has seeped into the colored notebooks; I think there will be no more black books; I think: It doesn't matter. There will be one single story, speaking with many voices, the one we are weaving together, they and I, about all that moves through us and that makes us what we are.

I go back to sit at my desk. I lay my field notebooks beside me, within reach. It is time. I start to write.

NASTASSJA MARTIN is a French author and anthropologist who has studied the Gwich'in people of Alaska and the Even people of the Kamchatka Peninsula. Along with *In the Eye of the Wild*, she has written *Les Âmes sauvages: Face à l'Occident, la résistance d'un peuple d'Alaska*, for which she received the Prix Louis Castex of the Académie Française.

SOPHIE R. LEWIS is an editor and a translator from French and Portuguese. Her translation of Noémi Lefebvre's *Blue Self-Portrait* was short-listed for both the Scott Moncrieff Prize and the Republic of Consciousness Prize in 2018.